GOLF

A Celebration of 100 years of the Rules of Play

GOLF

A Celebration of 100 years of the Rules of Play

Compiled by John Glover
Principal photographer David Cannon

MACMILLAN

Acknowledgements

A chance conversation between John Glover and David Cannon at the 1995 Walker Cup Match at Royal Porthcawl sparked off the idea of producing this magnificent book, which we are happy to adopt as part of our celebrations to mark the centenary of the formation of the Rules of Golf Committee.

I am therefore particularly grateful to both John and David not only for the idea but also for the immense amount of work which they have done in seeing the book through to fruition. John Glover has brought his wealth of golfing experience and his wonderful sense of humour into the words of the book, which is great fun to read. John has been ably assisted by his successor as Rules Secretary David Rickman, who has been a tower of strength in helping to shape and finalise the format of the book. The majority of the photographs were taken by David Cannon although these have been augmented by many of the other leading sports photographers at Allsport. The enormous task of researching the photographs was supervised by Andrew Redington.

However, to turn an idea into reality one requires the voice of experience and without the guidance of Ian and Marjory Chapman, we would not have known where to start. We pass on to them our grateful thanks not only for their ever-present support and advice but also for introducing us to the excellent designer Robert Updegraff and for their negotiations leading to our happy association with Macmillan who publish this book.

Finally, and by no means least, I would like to extend our appreciation to Royal & SunAlliance for the sponsorship of this book. We are most grateful for their continued support on many matters relating to the Rules of Golf.

David Pepper
CHAIRMAN, RULES OF GOLF COMMITTEE

First published 1997 by Macmillan
an imprint of Macmillan Publishers Ltd
25 Eccleston Place, London SW1W 9NF
and Basingstoke
Associated companies throughout the world

ISBN 0 333 71733 X

Copyright © The Royal and Ancient Golf Club

1 3 5 7 9 10 8 6 4 2

A CIP catalogue record for this book is available from the British Library.

Designed by Robert Updegraff
Picture research by Andrew Redington, Tim Matthews, Rupert Brooker and Paul Severn
Origination by Adelphi Graphics Limited
Printed and bound by Butler & Tanner Ltd, Frome and London

Picture Acknowledgements ALLSPORT UK All photographs by David Cannon except the following: Stephen Munday: 36 (above and below left), 37 (above right), 44 (above), 52/53, 65 (below), 68 (above), 69 (above), 70 (above), 72 (below) 74 (3), 75 (above), 79 (below), 90 (below), 93 (below), 94 (3), 102 (below), 118, 121 (below), 122 (below), 128 (above left), 161 (above), 172 (below). Andrew Redington: 56 (right), 70 (below right), 125 (left), 144 (above), 146, 147 (below), 148/149. Pascal Rondeau: 71 (below), 96 (below left), 133 (2), 151 (below). Phil Cole: 72 (above), 90 (above), 158/159. Graham Chadwick: 115, 147 (above) David Rogers: 66 Simon Bruty: 29 (above left and right), 38 (below), 67, 70 (above right), 75 (below), 93 (above), 111 (below), 151 (above), 152 (above and below left), 173 (below). Phil Inglis: 36 (below right), 106 (5). Anton Want: 104, 152 (below). Trevor Jones: 100 (below). Richard Saker: 60 (below), 69 (main). Howard Boylan: 84 (above left), 87 (above left), 126 (main), 139 (above). Michael Hobbs: 101 (below), 153 (right) Allsport UK Archive: 11 (left), 37 (above right), 48/49 (3). Allsport/Hulton Deutsch: 9, 40 (4), 42/43 (4), 46/47 (3), 54 (above (2) and below right), 120 (above).

ALLSPORT USA Stephen Dunn: 25 (below), 86 (below right), 102 (above 2), 108/109. Mike Powell: 63 (above), 128 (centre). J.D.Cuban: 27 (above), 34 (above), 35 (below), 50, 80 (left), 98, 124 (right), 136 (left 2), 137 (below). Jamie Squire: 35 (above). Gary Newkirk: 34 (below).

OTHER CONTRIBUTORS The Royal and Ancient Golf Club of St Andrews: 15 The United States Golf Association: 10 (above and below). John Glover: 136 (below right), 150 (all), 152 (below centre), 165 (below left), 172 (above), 176. Popperfoto: 87 (above right) Matthew Harris Golf Picture Library: 137 (above), 173 (above).

Extracts by Bernard Darwin from *Mostly Golf* and from various articles in *Country Life* are printed with the kind permission of A P Watt on behalf of Ursula Mommens, Lady Darwin and Dr Paul Ashton.

Half title photograph A Rules official examines Corey Pavin's ball in the edge of the bunker during the 1992 US Open at Pebble Beach.
Title spread photograph The Alfred Dunhill Cup, St Andrews, October 1995.

CONTENTS

Preface

In 1908, just 11 year after the formation of the Rules Committee, there began what is widely thought to be the longest running continuous commercial sponsorship of its kind in the world when Royal Insurance (now known as Royal SunAlliance) undertook to print the first indexed version of the Rules of Golf. The company continued to reprint the Rules when requested and in 1920 produced a larger format version for use in the Clubhouse.

Records do not show how many copies were initially printed but ninety years on some 3.6 million copies were distributed throughout Europe, the Middle and Far East, Africa and Australia including 2 million copies in UK and Ireland alone.

In 1996 Royal merged with Sun Alliance and on behalf of the new company I am pleased to continue an association of which we are enormously proud, via this publication. Through the closeness of our dealings with the R&A, my colleagues have gained the highest regard and respect for the people charged with maintaining the integrity of the game whilst developing the Rules in tune with the progress of the game itself. The spirit and conduct of play embodied in the Rules are exactly those qualities we in Royal SunAlliance aspire to in our dealings with customers, employees and the community at large throughout our worldwide operations – fairness and integrity.

It is therefore particularly fitting that we support the celebration of 100 years of the Rules Committee through our sponsorship of this illustrated Rules publication and of course the Rules themselves.

ROYAL & SUNALLIANCE

Richard Gamble
GROUP CHIEF EXECUTIVE
ROYAL SUNALLIANCE

I am pleased that it has been decided to recognise the centenary of the Rules of Golf Committee in the form of this commemorative book of stunning pictures on many aspects of the game.

At the time of the formation of the Rules of Golf Committee in 1897 amateur golf was booming and to this day, the amateur still remains at the heart of the game. During the last century we have witnessed great strides in the professional game which is now the shop window of golf, for it is evident that the professional and amateur games thrive on each other's success.

We are grateful to the professional golfers who helped to illustrate the Rules in the book, but the accompanying comment on the Rules of Golf is relevant to all who play the game throughout the world.

At its first meeting in 1898 the Committee, strangely enough, considered a Rules query from Senekal Golf Club in my homeland South Africa. One hundred years on and the Committee continues to receive queries on the Rules of Golf from around the world.

Why do we play golf? Possibly it is for companionship, but I believe golf's greatest attraction lies in its being a game for all ages, played in most parts of the world in an unending variety of terrain and condition, from well-nigh perfect to downright inhospitable.

It requires the greatest self discipline and for the most part it is the player on his own, who has to cope with every challenge that confronts him. Essentially this responsibility relates equally to the Rules of Golf, where it is for the individual to apply the Rules to his own situation before requesting confirmation from his opponent or fellow-competitor or ultimately a referee.

What the future will bring is anyone's guess, but I look forward with confidence and optimism. The Rules must keep abreast of modern times, without stifling innovation or intimidating manufacturers. The challenge will be to retain a balance between fairness and the traditions, in a framework that encompasses the all-important spirit of the game.

My grateful thanks to the many people who over the years have willingly devoted much of their leisure time to the study of the Rules, so that those of us who play this great game can do so under a just and respected code. Enjoy your golf.

T Harvey Douglas
CAPTAIN

On behalf of American golfers, I congratulate the Rules of Golf Committee of the Royal and Ancient Golf Club of St Andrews on the occasion of its centenary.

Fidelity to golf's rules is an acquired skill, in that it takes time, effort and experience to learn the code. This book, produced to honour the R&A's dedication to the Rules of Golf, offers wonderful observations that will help any student of the Rules. Beautifully illustrated with photographs and artfully bound, it will be a treasure in the library of anyone who loves the game.

At the same time, any small and simple copy of the current Rules of Golf is the greatest testament to the enduring bond between the R&A and the United States Golf Association. For more than 100 years, we have shared the joys of golf. Once the game became popular in the United States, players from our nations criss-crossed the Atlantic to compete in our respective national championships. Additionally, since 1922, our finest amateurs have enjoyed the mutual friendships fostered by the Walker Cup Match and, since 1932, the Curtis Cup Match.

Today the code – created by our combined and continuing efforts – is observed wherever the game is played.

The relationship between your Committee and ours endures and our work continues. The bond is strong, the friendship true.

Judy Bell
PRESIDENT

The warning sign on 'Granny Clarke's Wynd' the road that crosses the 18th and 1st fairways of the Old Course at St Andrews.

Introduction

GOLF IS NOT A FUNERAL BUT BOTH CAN BE SAD AFFAIRS.

Bernard Darwin, Chairman, Rules Committee 1946–49

HOW IT ALL BEGAN

St Andrews has long been known as the home of golf. When it was founded in 1754, the R&A was described – somewhat quaintly – as 'the Alma Mater of the Golf'. Since that time the Club has evolved through two and a half centuries as golf's senior authority.

The history of the R&A is inextricably tied to that of the ancient city of St Andrews where golf was believed to be a popular sport when the university was founded in 1413. By 1457 the game had gained such popularity that James II banned it, together with football, because able-bodied men from the townships were neglecting their archery practice in favour of these other sports.

The status of the R&A as being the leading authority was officially recognised in 1897 when the explosive growth of the game led to a general demand for a uniform code of Rules. Previously the Club had issued a code of Rules for St Andrews and these Rules were applied by the majority of other clubs, but each was free to follow or ignore these laws.

The vital need for an overall Rules authority finally set in motion a movement which led to a formal plea for unity from the senior Clubs which ran the Amateur Championship. The R&A was approached to evolve a scheme which would result in national recognition of one code of Rules.

On 28th September 1897, the R&A nominated a committee of fifteen of its own members to be known as the Rules of Golf Committee. This action propelled the Club into being the established governing authority with well defined powers. Even today the R&A does not impose the Rules of Golf but rather governs by consent.

With the exception of the USA, whose allegiance lies with the United States Golf Association, and Canada which is self-governing but affiliated to the R&A, every country which has taken up this ancient game accepts the Club's authority over the laws of the game and also the regulations on Amateur Status. There are, in fact, over one hundred countries affiliated to the R&A.

The 17th green on the Old Course at St Andrews at the turn of the century.

9

AGREEMENT ACROSS THE ATLANTIC

By 1950 the Rules of the R&A and USGA were drifting further apart even though there was liaison between the two bodies, and so a meeting was held in 1951. The following is an extract from an article written by Joe Dey, a Past Captain of the R&A and former Executive Director of the USGA.

'Twelve men sat around a large conference table. They were in a committee room of the House of Lords in London. The twelve men represented the governing authorities of golf in Great Britain, Australia, Canada and the United States. They were trying to develop a code of Rules of Golf which could be used uniformly throughout the world. In the main, this meant trying to reconcile the differences between the British and American codes, in substance and form.

'At the moment of which we write, the conferees were in deep discussion of a point. After full consideration the British view prevailed. At lunch the R&A representatives decided it would be preferable to change their position because of possible complications for the USGA. "That", said Lord Brabazon of Tara, "is the way to negotiate: you win your point and then concede it."'

After much discussion the meeting produced a uniform code of Rules that came into use throughout the world in 1952.

Perhaps the most major change at that time was the demise of the beloved stymie. Accordingly, players in a match are no longer required to play around or chip

Julius Boros, winner of the 1952 US Open, the first US Open to be played under the new uniform code of Rules.

over an opponent's ball coming to rest between their ball and the hole. Not long ago a journalist telephoned the R&A and by mistake was put through to the bar. He enquired when the stymie had been abolished and was promptly told that it hadn't been because there is a bottle on the shelf and we still serve it!

The minimum size of the golf ball is the only debate which has caused disharmony since. That final difference of opinion disappeared with the demise of the small 1.62 inch ball on 1st January 1990 and acceptance of the 1.68 inch ball.

MODERN TIMES

The R&A and the USGA meet twice annually to discuss the revision of clauses which are then reviewed at length with both amateur and professional golfing bodies worldwide. Any agreed changes in the Rules of Golf are made every four years.

The headquarters of the United States Golf Association in Far Hills, New Jersey.

The present day Rules of Golf Committee is made up of twelve members of the R&A and up to a further twelve representatives of golfing bodies at home and abroad. The USGA were first represented in 1907 and there are also advisory members from Britain's Council of National Golf Unions and the Ladies' Golf Union, plus delegates from Europe, Australia, New Zealand, Canada, South Africa, South America, Asia and the Pacific and Japan.

The Committee will only consider enquiries from clubs and governing bodies, not from individuals. Key points raised in the queries received by the R&A and in the United States are selected for inclusion in the annually published bible for Rules Committees everywhere – Decisions on the Rules of Golf. Each volume contains over 1,000 Decisions, which assist in a consistent interpretation of the Rules throughout the world.

The Committee is asked some extraordinary questions. A lady wrote to the R&A stating that she would not bore the Committee with the facts but could it

The present Rules Secretary of the R&A David Rickman on duty on the 11th green with Leroy Ritchie of the USGA at the 1996 Masters tournament.

help her concerning a match which she had won at the 17th but then lost at the 21st! A man asked the Committee to settle a bet about a matter which was causing him much unhappiness and had divided the club down the middle. He related the case and concluded by saying that if the Committee did not agree with him, then please do not reply! The nine 'How would you rule?' cases in this book have all been submitted to the R&A. The answers are listed separately on page 192 to give readers time to think about them before reading the official decision.

Judgements made by the R&A on the Rules of Golf, the acceptable design of clubs and balls and countless other aspects of golf which affect every player from the newest recruit to the championship winner, are made against the history of the game, but also always with an understanding of modern demands.

Since the first Rules Committee of 1897, the R&A has spawned two further Committees; one body to rule specifically on the admissibility or otherwise of new clubs and golf balls and another to rule on Amateur Status.

This book traces how it all began in the eighteenth century, to the present day. We share fascinating detail of how the Rules have changed, with anecdotes that are often hilarious. The current code is explained (with appropriate references detailed for those who want to know more) and it is all brought to life through the lens of a camera. The glorious illustrations are a feast to the eye and will delight the imagination.

The current Secretary of the R&A Michael Bonallack playing at Royal Troon in 1970.

THE FIRST CODE

The first written Rules of Golf were drawn up in 1744 by The Gentlemen Golfers of Leith and these thirteen 'Articles & Laws in the Playing at Golf' were adopted with one minor change of procedure, by The Society of St Andrews Golfers, in 1754.

Articles and Laws in Playing the Golf

(St Andrews, 14th May 1754)

I.   You must Tee your Ball within a Club length of the Hole.

II.   Your Tee must be upon the ground.

III.   You are not to change the Ball which you strike off the Tee.

IV.   You are not to remove Stones, Bones, or any Break-club for the sake of playing your Ball, except upon the fair Green, and that only within a Club length of your Ball.

V.   If your Ball come among Watter, or any Wattery filth, you are at liberty to take out your Ball and throw it behind the hazard, six yards at least; you may play it with any club, and allow your Adversary a stroke for so getting out your Ball.

VI.   If your Balls be found anywhere touching one another, you are to lift the first Ball till you play the last.

VII.   At holing, you are to play your Ball honestly for the Hole, and not to play upon your Adversary's Ball, not lying in your way to the Hole.

VIII. If you should lose your Ball by its being taken up, or in any other way, you are to go back to the spot where you struck last, and drop another Ball, and allow your Adversary a stroke for the misfortune.

IX.   No man, at Holing his Ball, is to be allowed to mark to the Hole with his Club or anything else.

X.   If a Ball be stop'd by any person, Horse, Dog, or anything else, the Ball so stopped must be played where it lies.

XI.   If you draw your Club in order to strike, and proceed so far in the stroke as to be bringing down your Club – if then your Club shall break in any way it is to be accounted a stroke.

XII.   He whose Ball lyes farthest from the Hole is obliged to play first.

XIII. Neither Trench, Ditch, nor Dyke made for the preservation of the Links, nor the Scholars' holes, nor the Soldiers' lines, shall be accounted a Hazard, but the Ball is to be taken out, Teed, and played with any iron Club.

THE 1812 CODE

It has been said that the Rules of Golf are simple – that is until you do something you are not supposed to do!

In the early days the Rules only dealt with 'match play' and the principles were very simple. If you infringed a Rule, you lost the hole and walked to the next tee. Also the old adage of 'Play the ball where it lies' reflected the spirit of the game in those days and if for some reason you could not play the ball 'as it lay', you put it in your pocket and 'gave up' the hole.

There were only two exceptions to the principle that the ball must not be touched by hand during the play of a hole and those were because of the nature of the ground on which the original game was played. A 'Break-club', a large pebble or similar obstacle, might if within a club-length of the ball, be removed without penalty. Similarly a ball might be lifted from 'Wattery Filth', which is the slime left by a receding tide – penalty one stroke. There was no provision for a 'lost ball', a 'ball out of bounds' (regarded as lost) or a ball which was 'unplayable'.

As the game evolved Societies and (later) Clubs made there own Rules. Although St Andrews was not the oldest of these Societies it became the acknowledged authority on the Laws and regulations of the game.

The code of seventeen Rules and Regulations, below, was framed in 1812 by the 'Society of St. Andrews Golfers' for its own use and remains the basis on which today's Rules are structured.

Regulations for the Game of Golf

Adopted By The St Andrew's Society Of Golfers,
At their Meeting, Friday 1st May, 1812.

I THE Balls must be teed not nearer the hole than two club-lengths, nor further than four.

II THE Ball farthest from the hole must be played first.

III THE Ball struck from the tee must not be changed before the hole is played out, and if the parties are at a loss to know the one Ball from the other, neither shall be lifted till both parties agree.

IV STONES, Bones, or any break-club within a club-length of the Ball may be removed when the Ball lies on grass, but nothing can be removed if it lies on Sand or in a bunker, if however it Stick fast in the ground, it may be loosened.

V IF the Ball lie in a Rabbit-scrape, the Player shall not be at liberty to take it out, but must play it as from any common hazard, if however it lie in one of the burrows, he may lift it, drop it behind the hazard, and play with an iron without losing a stroke.

VI IF the Ball is half covered or more with water, the Player may take it out, tee it, and play from behind the hazard, losing a stroke.

VII   IF the Ball lie in the supernumerary hole on the hole-across green, it may be dropped behind the hazard, and played with an Iron, without losing a stroke.

VIII   WHEN the Balls lie within six inches of one another, the Ball nearest the hole must be lifted till the other is played, but on the putting green it shall not be lifted, although within six inches, unless it be directly between the other and the hole.

IX WHATEVER happens to a Ball by accident, must be reckoned a Rub of the green, if however, the Player's Ball strike his adversary or his Cady, the adversary loses the hole: If it strike his own Cady, the Player loses the hole: If the Player strike his adversary's Ball with his Club, the Player loses the hole.

X IF a Ball is lost, the stroke goes for nothing, the Player returns to the spot whence the ball was struck, tees it, and loses a stroke.

XI IF in striking, the Club breaks, it is nevertheless to be counted a stroke, if the Player either strike the ground or pass the Ball.

XII IN holing, you are not to place any mark to direct you to the hole, you are to play your Ball fairly and honestly for the hole, and not on your adversary's Ball not lying in your way to the hole.

XIII   ALL loose impediments of whatever kind, may be removed upon the putting green.

XIV   IN all cases where a Ball is to be dropped, the party dropping shall front the hole to which he is playing, and drop the Ball behind him, over his head.

XV   WHEN a Ball is completely covered with fog, bent, whins &c. so much thereof shall be set aside as that the Player shall have a full view of his Ball before he plays.

XVI   WHEN the Balls touch each other, one of them must be lifted until the other is played.

XVII   ANY disputes respecting the play shall be determined by the Captain or Senior Member present, and if none of the Members are present, by the Captain and his annual Council for the time.

Royal and Ancient Golf Club of St Andrews

Resolution as to appointment of Rules of Golf Committee

That:

1. The Club appoint a Committee, consisting of fifteen members, who shall be called the Rules of Golf Committee. Six members shall form a quorum, and the Chairman, who shall be appointed at the first meeting of the Committee, shall, in case of equality, have a casting as well as a deliberative vote.

2. That the Committee shall consist of the following members:-

L. M. Balfour Melville	R. A. Hull
Ernley R. H. Blackwell	C. Hutchings
B. Hall Blyth	H. G. Hutchinson
Captain Burn	J. E. Laidlay
H. S. Colt	J. L. Low
H. S. C. Everard	R. B. Sharp
J. O. Fairlie	F. G. Tait
S. Mure Fergusson	

3. The powers of the Committee shall be limited to dealing with proposals relating to, or questions of interpretation arising on the Rules and Customs of the Game of Golf. On all questions of interpretation of the Rules they shall be the final authority.

4. Any resolution to amend or repeal an existing rule, or make a new rule, must be carried by a majority of the members of the Committee present and voting at a meeting; but such resolution shall not be operative until it has been passed by a majority of not less than two-thirds of the members present at a General Meeting of the Club.

5. Any such resolution of the Committee shall be communicated to the Hon Secretary of the Club, who shall give notice of it in the usual way, a fortnight before the half-yearly meeting at which it is to be submitted.

6. The Committee shall meet at least twice a year, two of the meetings to be held during the weeks of the Spring and Autumn Meetings, on days to be fixed by the Chairman, who shall cause notice thereof to be sent to each member at least seven days before the date fixed.

7. The Committee shall hold office for three years, and the new Committee shall be elected by ballot at the Autumn Meeting occurring at the expiry of that term. Vacancies occurring during the three years shall be filled by the Committee, but members so placed on the Committee shall cease to hold office at the same time as the other members of the Committee. Members of the Committee shall be eligible for re-election. Members proposing candidates for the Committee shall do so by lists, signed by the proposer and seconder, to be transmitted to the Secretary of the Club one month before the Autumn meeting. The names contained in such lists shall be printed in an alphabetical list, and posted in the Club House. Members present at the Autumn Meeting shall be supplied with a copy of the list, and shall give their votes by placing a cross opposite the names of not more than fifteen of the candidates in the list. Lists so marked shall be placed in a box (which shall be provided at the door) before the members leave the meeting. Those having the largest number of votes shall form the Committee. No voting paper shall be valid which is marked in any other way than by crosses, or which has crosses opposite more names than fifteen. The Captain of the Club, or, in his absence, the Chairman at the General Meeting, shall be the scrutineer of the votes, and he shall make out and sign a list of the Committee, which shall be posted in the Club House on the evening of the day on which the ballot is taken. He shall also fix the date on which the first meeting of the Committee shall take place, and make the necessary arrangements for calling the Committee together for that meeting.

8. The Committee shall appoint a Secretary, who shall keep minutes of the meetings, and attend to correspondence addressed to the Committee.

9. A copy of any decision of the Committee dealing with the interpretation of the existing Rules of Golf shall be posted in the Club House for one month.

28th September, 1897.

THE 1899 CODE

The first code to be issued, after the formation of the Rules of Golf Committee of the R&A, appeared in 1899 and it contained many of the variations which had applied in other Golfing Societies and Clubs throughout the British Isles. It was the first code which contained a section on 'etiquette'.

The Rules would be revised again in 1903, 1908, 1912 and 1921 when, to avoid delay, the play of a 'provisional ball', was approved.

As time went on it was generally accepted that it 'be fair' to allow a player to proceed under penalty, rather than pocket his ball, when a ball had landed 'out of bounds', was 'lost' or became 'unplayable'. In stroke play, when the player found himself in some 'difficulty' he was allowed to tee a ball any distance behind the spot and add two penalty strokes to his score for that hole.

These changes were well received by the growing numbers of people playing golf many of whom might not have persevered, as beginners, under the principle of 'play the ball or pocket it'.

THE 1984 CODE

The Rules, which became effective on 1st April 1984, represented the first comprehensive revision since international uniformity was achieved in 1952. The revision was based on a proposal which had been circulated to golfing bodies around the world in 1981 for which strong support was received. In revising the Rules the R&A and the USGA attempted, where feasible, to simplify them as well and it was hoped that they would be easier to learn and apply. To achieve uniformity of interpretation of the Rules, the R&A and the USGA combined their two decisions services into a single completely re-written decisions service, which became available for worldwide reference early in 1984.

A photograph of the Quadrennial Rules Conference, May 1983, features on page 192.

MILESTONES IN RULES HISTORY

1744 First written code of Rules. Rule 1 stated: 'You must tee your ball within a club length of the hole.'

1850 With the introduction of the gutty ball a new Rule provided that if a ball broke up in flight another ball could be dropped without penalty where the largest piece was found.

1897 Formation of the R&A Rules of Golf Committee.

1904 Time allowed in searching for a ball was reduced from 10 to 5 minutes.
The 'putting green' defined as all ground within 20 yards of the hole, except hazards.

1922 Limitations were first imposed on the weight and size of the golf ball in an attempt to limit the distance it would travel.

1929 Steel shafts were permitted for the first time.

1939 Only fourteen clubs to be carried from this date.

1949 The playing of a provisional ball for an unplayable ball no longer permitted.
The penalty for all breaches of Rule, except those which may be regarded as deliberate, is one stroke in both match play and stroke play. The penalty for 'out of bounds', 'unplayable ball' and 'lost ball' reduced from stroke and distance to distance only. Traditional penalties were restored in 1952.
Committees were empowered to disqualify players who unduly delayed others. Modified in 1952 to loss of hole or a two-stroke penalty, and for repeated offences, disqualification.

1952 First worldwide unified code of Rules agreed and the stymie abolished.
Score card to be countersigned by the competitor.

1960 Distance measuring devices banned.

1968 Stableford System: In 1931, Dr Stableford, a surgeon in Wallasey, devised a points system because he felt that a player's score should reflect his play and not be ruined by one bad hole. Although it proved a success it took 37 years to convince the Rules Committee.

1984 Ball no longer dropped over the player's shoulder, but at arm's length and at shoulder height.

1990 The 1.68 inch ball becomes the only legal ball. Final demise of the small 'British' ball.

1996 First mention of the words 'Slow Play'.

THE GAME

YOU HAVE TO BE A LITTLE CRAZY TO PLAY GOLF,
BUT YOU'RE MAD IF YOU DON'T.

HENEVER YOU SET OUT to play golf, you have three opponents – yourself, the course and the other man. You might even have a fourth – the game itself. Indeed, to the newcomer this will at first be the stiffest opponent of the four.

Henry Longhurst

The basic principle of golf of hitting a ball from one point to another in as few strokes as you can has not changed since the game started some five hundred years ago. The golfer may complain that the weather is too hot or too cold; the course is too wet or too dry; or the greens are too fast or too slow. He can point the blame at almost anything except himself - but that's his privilege.

The Definitions section of the Rule book is most important as these carefully defined terms form the foundation around which the Rules of Play are written. Some alternative Definitions are as follows:

Golf An incurable disease (common to both sexes), generally fatal to the middle aged.
Par The scratch score for any hole; so called because you have only the ghost of a chance of making it.
Hole A small depression in the green; frequently the cause of much depression.
Good Lie A convincing explanation.
Driver A wooden or metal headed tool intended to give length without breadth.
Clubhead So called because it is at the foot of the club.
Sand Iron Iron tool for removing the bunker from the ball.
Putter A mathematical tool for playing the last four strokes of each hole.
Putt Originally a shot along the ground near the hole. Some players, however, take their putt first.
Bye That part of the match at which you really begin to get on your game.

The mental torture of golf can, perhaps, be summed up by the following statement: 'I didn't play my normal game today. Come to think of it, I never play my normal game!'

Opposite The Valley Course at Royal Portrush Golf Club, Northern Ireland. 'Lowery like' figures stretch out across the links late on a stormy summer's evening.

17

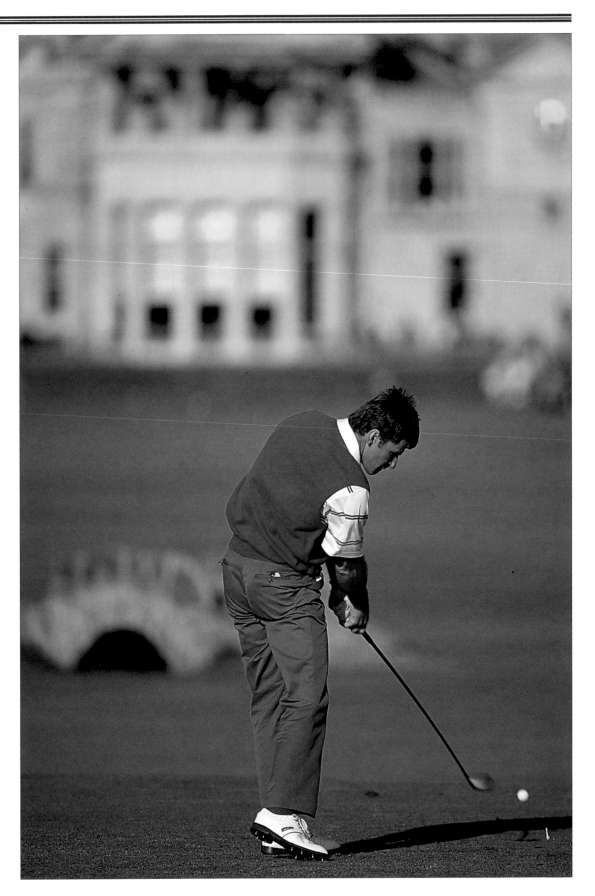

Nick Faldo driving from the 18th tee of the Old Course, St Andrews, during the 1990 Open Championship.

Rule 1-1 'The Game of Golf consists in playing a ball from the 'teeing ground'…

'Calamity' Royal Portrush
14th hole 200 yards par3.

A good American player, on his first visit to Portrush, walked on to the 14th tee and was faced with a strong wind from the left.

'Say, how am I going to play this one?' he enquired of his caddie.

His caddie was quick to reply, 'Well, you hit a high hook that straightens out and then fades on to the green.'

'But how do I do that?' asked the player.

His caddie answered, 'You should know, that's the way you've been playing all morning.'

And if 'Calamity' is not enough to try one's patience the next hole is aptly named 'Purgatory'.

'The game of golf, if I may write for the uninitiated, is essentially a business of starting here and finishing there, overcoming as best you may all the hazards encountered on the way and endeavouring to get your ball into the hole in fewer strokes than the other man.'

Henry Longhurst

Pine Valley 10th hole par 3.   A past captain of the R&A played his first stroke in North America at Pine Valley's 10th hole and holed in one. When he was later recounting the story he was asked if he had had the ball mounted.

    'No' he replied 'I lost it at the next hole!'

… into the hole by a 'stroke' or successive strokes in accordance with the Rules.

Seve Ballesteros birdies the 18th hole to secure the 1984 Open Championship at St Andrews.

The competitor who plays the 'stipulated round' or rounds in the fewest strokes is the winner. (Rule 3-1)

The 'stipulated round' consists of playing the holes of the course in their correct sequence unless otherwise authorised by the Committee. The number of holes in a stipulated round is 18 unless a smaller number is authorised by the Committee. (Definition)

21

Cypress Point 15th hole one of two consecutive par-3s. Robert Louis Stevenson
once described the Monterey Peninsula, California, on whose shores lie Pebble Beach
and Cypress Point, as 'the greatest meeting place of land and water in the world'.

The world's leading players compete annually for the four 'Majors' - the Masters, the US Open, the Open Championship and the USPGA Championship.

These are stroke play events and each consists of 4 rounds of 18 holes. In the event of a tie after 72 holes, the Masters and USPGA have a sudden-death play-off, the Open Championship has a 4-hole play-off and the US Open has an 18-hole play-off. (See Decision 33-6/2)

Above The 17th green at Augusta National in the late evening, home of the Masters Tournament.

Right Tom Kite plays his second shot to the 9th hole during the final round of the 1991 US Open at Pebble Beach.

Left The Red Arrows join in the celebration of Nick Faldo's victory in the 1990 Open Championship at St Andrews.

Below The fans salute Steve Elkington's winning putt as he defeats Colin Montgomerie in the play-off for the 1994 USPGA Championship at the Riviera Club, Los Angeles.

A competition is deemed to have closed when the result has been officially announced. (Rule 34-1b)

Two of the most sought after Amateur titles in the men's game are for the British and the United States Amateur Championships.

Both Championships consist of two rounds of stroke play after which the leading 64 players qualify for the match play stage.

In stroke play qualifying followed by match play, a competition is deemed to have closed when the player has teed off in his first match. (Rule 34-1b)

The essential difference between match play and stroke play is that in match play only you and your opponent are involved, whereas in stroke play every competitor has an interest in the results of your play.

Right Warren Bladon with the Amateur Championship trophy.

Below Warren Bladon holes his birdie putt at the 18th hole on the Ailsa Course, Turnberry, to win the 1996 Amateur Championship.

Above Tiger Woods and the US Amateur trophy. He won the US Amateur title in three successive years, 1994-96.

Right Tiger Woods took the 1997 Masters by a record 12-stroke margin, becoming the youngest competitor to win the title.

The players in a match are the only parties involved and may therefore do as they see fit in taking or not taking action to protect their rights. For example, in match play, when a player starts the play of a hole by playing his ball from outside the teeing ground, the opponent may require the player to cancel the stroke and play a ball from within the teeing ground, without penalty. (Rule 11-4a)

In stroke play, since the Rules must protect the rights of all the absent competitors, the competitor has no option and is required to replay the stroke from within the teeing ground under penalty of two strokes. (Rule 11-4b)

This does not mean that in match play the players may actually agree to disregard the Rules. A generous player may overlook a Rules infringement by his opponent, but if this is done by mutual agreement then neither player is playing the game properly and both should be removed from the competition. (Rule 1-3)

THE RYDER CUP

First played in 1927 between teams from Great Britain and the United States, the Ryder Cup is now competed for every two years by European and American teams. The three-day match consists of 8 foursomes, 8 four-balls and 12 singles.

A 'foursome' is a match in which two play against two, and each side plays one ball. (Rule 29)
A 'four-ball' is a match in which two play their better ball against the better ball of two other players. (Rule 30)
A 'partner' is a player associated with another player on the same side. (Definition)
During a 'stipulated round' a player shall not give 'advice' to anyone in the competition except his partner. A player may ask for advice during a stipulated round from only his partner or either of their caddies. (Rule 8-1)

Left Seve Ballesteros and Jose Maria Olazabal have been regular partners in the foursomes and four-ball matches.

Centre Bernhard Langer suffers as his putt to retain the trophy for Europe in 1991 at Kiawah Island slides past the hole.

Right Sam Torrance celebrates holing the putt that secured Europe's victory in 1985.

Left Hale Irwin is swamped by celebrating players and fans alike after the US victory at Kiawah Island in 1991.

Below Philip Walton is lifted by Europe's Captain Bernard Gallacher after he had secured the vital point against Jay Haas to win the 1995 match.

Foot of page Ian Woosnam leads the European celebrations at Oak Hill in 1995.

THE WALKER CUP

The Walker Cup Match between Amateur golfers from Great Britain and Ireland and the United States of America has been played 35 times since its institution in 1922.

The two-day match, which is held every two years, consists of 8 foursomes and 16 singles.

In a foursome, during any 'stipulated round' the partners shall play alternately from the teeing grounds and alternately during the play of each hole. Penalty strokes do not affect the order of play. (Rule 29-1)

Main Tiger Woods plays his second shot to the 18th at Royal Porthcawl in 1995. His ball came to rest out of bounds and he lost his first day match to Gary Wolstenholme.

Inset Tiger Woods congratulates Gary Wolstenholme on his one hole victory.

Inset opposite The victorious 1995 Great Britain and Ireland team.

HOW WOULD YOU RULE?

In a foursome, whose turn is it to play if your partner has an airshot with the opponent's ball?

THE SOLHEIM CUP

Although the Solheim Cup only dates back to 1990 this match, between the women professional golfers of Europe and the United States of America, has quickly established itself as the equivalent of the men's Ryder Cup.

Right Members of the European team run to congratulate Catrin Nilsmark on holing the putt to win the 1992 Match at Dalmahoy.

32

Below American celebrations at St Pierre in 1996.

THE CURTIS CUP

The Curtis Cup, a match between women Amateur golfers from Great Britain and Ireland and the United States of America, is the women's equivalent of the Walker Cup.

Left The Great Britain and Ireland team celebrates beside the lake at Killarney Golf and Fishing Club in Ireland having won the 1996 match.

Above Kelli Kuehne holes a birdie putt during the 1996 match. The American may have finished on the losing side in the Curtis Cup, but the following week she won the British Ladies Amateur Championship.

The Committee may, in the conditions of a team competition (Rule 33-1), permit each team to appoint one person who may give advice (including pointing out a line for putting) to members of that team. The Committee may lay down conditions relating to the appointment and permitted conduct of such person, who must be identified to the Committee before giving advice.

THE PRESIDENT'S CUP

A new addition to the world of team golf is the 'President's Cup' – a match played every two years between the United States of America and a team from the rest of the world, excluding Europe. Already the matches are hailed a success and have given players such as Greg Norman, Ernie Els, Nick Price and Jumbo Ozaki a chance to play match play team golf as professionals. The USA have managed to win the first two matches, though in 1996 it was by the narrowest of margins.

Above Mark McNulty from Zimbabwe together with Australian Greg Norman and South African David Frost share in the excitement of the President's Cup.

Right The victorious American team after the 1994 Match.

Left Fred Couples holes his match winning putt against Vijay Singh in 1996.

Below Arnold Palmer takes a happy look sideways as his team celebrate their dramatic last gasp victory in the 1996 matches at the Robert Trent Jones Golf Club, Lake Manassas, Virginia.

THE FRUSTRATIONS OF THE GAME

'Golf being a cold, calculating sort of game gives perhaps more scope for folly than any other. We have all the time in the world to make up our minds as to what is the wise thing to do and then to do the foolish one.'

Bernard Darwin

Above Joakim Haegmann reflects on a foolish act at the 1994 Volvo Masters at Valderrama, Spain.

Above right Brad Faxon cannot believe his putt on the 17th green missed during the final round of the 1995 USPGA Championship at the Riviera Club in Los Angeles.

Below Greg Norman falls in despair beside the 15th green as the 1996 Masters Tournament slips from his grasp.

Below right Tommy Horton tries to coax his ball into the hole at the 1993 British Seniors Championship at Royal Lytham & St Annes.

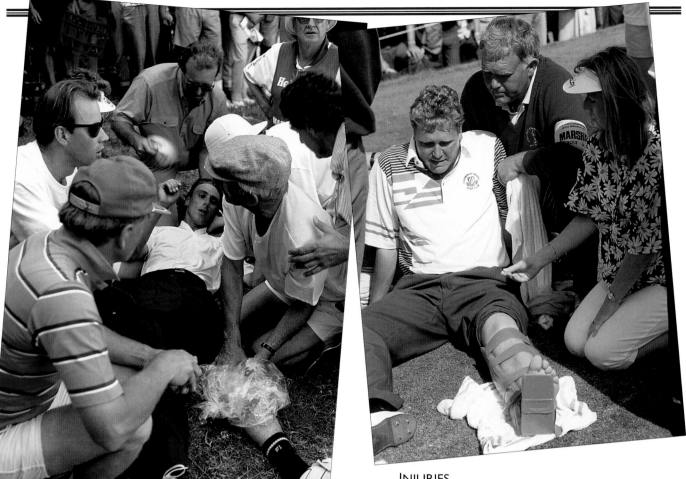

Injuries

Top left In the last round of the 1990 Australian Open, Brett Ogle was just two shots off the lead playing the 17th hole. His second shot, with a 2-iron, hit a tree immediately in front of him and his ball came straight back and struck him on the knee. Apart from being extremely painful he suffered the further indignity of a penalty of two strokes because the ball had hit him (Rule 19-2). The hole cost him a 9 and any chance of winning the title.

It would be reasonable to allow a player 10-15 minutes to recuperate from such a physical problem but ordinarily allowing more time than that would be inadvisable. (Decision 6-8a/3)

Above Richard Boxall was forced to discontinue play at the 9th tee during the 1991 Open Championship at Royal Birkdale because of a fracture in his leg.

Left Ian Woosnam became ill during the 1992 Johnnie Walker Classic in Bangkok and needed oxygen on course.

A player is permitted to 'discontinue play' if there is a good reason, such as sudden illness. (Rule 6-8a)

DISTRACTIONS

Distractions are a common occurrence which players must accept as a part of the game. (Decision 1-4/1)

Above The 1st hole at Prestwick Golf Club, Scotland and adjacent railway line.

If a passing train distracts a player, causing him to miss-hit his shot, that is his misfortune. He is not entitled to replay the stroke without penalty.

Right Pat Bradley tries to concentrate on her game despite her feathered friends.

Most golf courses have a large variety of resident wildlife. Whilst playing in such natural surroundings is part of the attraction of the game, it does mean that occasional distractions are inevitable.

A bird is an 'animate outside agency'. The distraction of a bird on the ground, or in flight, is something the player must accept.

If a player's ball comes to rest in a bird's nest he may, in equity (Rule 1-4), without penalty, drop a ball at the nearest spot not nearer the hole which would allow him to make his stroke without damaging the nest. If the ball lies in a hazard it must be dropped in the hazard. (Decision 1-4/9)

Paul Affleck is dwarfed by the aircraft landing behind him as he plays from the 7th tee at Tanah Merah Country Club, Singapore.

Many golf courses are situated adjacent or close to airports and players must simply ignore the passing air traffic.

HOW WOULD YOU RULE?

As a player swung his club there was an earthquake, measuring 7.1 on the Richter scale, causing him to hit his ball out of bounds. May the player cancel the stroke and replay it, without penalty?

THE PLAYERS

GOLF IS A GAME FOR ALL AGES , MALE AND FEMALE,
WITH ONE SET OF RULES FOR AMATEUR AND PROFESSIONAL ALIKE.

I T WAS THE INAUGURATION of the British Amateur Championship in 1885 that first created a need to define an 'amateur'. Entries for this event were not accepted from those who had played for prize money in 'open' events, nor from club and ball makers, those who taught golf for payment or caddies. In 1897 the Rules were revised whereupon course architects and greenkeepers and anyone who played against a professional for a money bet or stake were ruled out of the amateur game. Much has changed since the early days, but it is clear that the principles of Amateur Status were established a long time ago.

Golf is unique in having a strong professional game and a strong amateur game. The world of the tournament golfer is the shop window of golf as can be seen from the photographs in this book. Tournament professionals are dependant for their living on television audiences, and on those people who form the market for the goods and services sold by their sponsors. Club professionals earn their living by teaching and selling equipment. For both, the amateur golfer is essential.

But what of the amateur golfer? Because golf has a handicapping system he or she can compete on fair terms with a player of any standard. Amateurs can play with whomever, whenever and wherever they wish.

A few years ago the R&A received a query from Ireland asking whether a Life Assurance Policy was a valid prize. It was intended that the policy would provide a sum at death only, with no surrender value. The question was whether it could be construed under the Rules to be equivalent to prize money. Although the R&A did not believe that there was any breach of the Rules, it decided to ask the United States Golf Association for its view. The following is the final paragraph of the response.

'We are of one mind on a critical point. If the prize winner should become deceased during the term of the policy he must surely be stripped of Amateur Status'.

Amateurs play the game for fun. 'Not so' some say.

Opposite
(Top insets Left to Right)
Jamie Anderson, Old Tom Morris, Young Tom Morris;
(Main Picture Left to Right)
Alex Herd, James Braid, J. H. Taylor and Harry Vardon.

Bobby Jones is the only golfer to have won the British and American Amateur and Open Championships in the same year – 1930. The closest Jones came to defeat in these four Championships was in his match against Cyril Tolley in the British Amateur Championship. Tolley has written that in the course of the match and in the absence of crowd control, spectators were hit nine times in all by Jones's ball and five times by his own. The match ended at the 19th hole and took the unprecedented time of four hours and twenty-five minutes.

If a ball in motion is accidentally deflected or stopped by an 'outside agency', it is a 'rub of the green', no penalty is incurred and the ball shall be played as it lies. (Rule 19-1)

Above Bobby Jones, one of only three amateur golfers to win the Open Championship, drives from the 17th tee on the Old Course during the 1927 Open at St Andrews.

Right Bobby Jones with the Open Trophy in 1927. He also won in 1926 and 1930.

Walter Hagen has a remarkable record in the Open Championship. He played in eight championships, and in addition to winning four times, he finished second in 1923 and third in 1926.

Left Walter Hagen dressed in his normal extravagant attire being filmed at the Open at Sandwich in 1928.

Below Walter Hagen plays the 7th hole at Royal Troon in the 1923 Open Championship.

The 1923 Open at Royal Troon was marked by a controversy involving the iron clubs of a number of American professionals. It was claimed that protruding ragged pieces of metal on the club face allowed excessive backspin to be imparted to the ball. Files were borrowed from local shipyards to smooth the clubfaces to an acceptable level.

The face of the club shall be hard and rigid (some exceptions may be made for putters) and, except for markings as permitted by Appendix II, shall be smooth and shall not have any degree of concavity. (Rule 4-1e)

Gene Sarazen travelled to Prince's in Kent for the 1932 Open Championship with a new club in his bag. He had come to the conclusion that his bunker play was not as good as it should be and he disliked the thin-edged niblicks commonly used at that time. Accordingly, he added a flange to the back of the club and so the sand wedge was invented. His success at getting up and down from the bunkers at Prince's helped him win the Championship by five shots.

Left Gene Sarazen, the first player to win all four 'major' titles – the Masters, the US Open, the Open and the USPGA.

Below Gene Sarazen and Sam Snead, Honorary Starters at the Masters, on the 1st tee at Augusta in 1984.

44

Sam Snead won the Open Championship in 1946, the first Championship to be played since 1939 because of the outbreak of World War II.

For those who did try to play golf during these times there were unusual difficulties. To meet the conditions the following 'Rules' were written by Major G L Edsell, Secretary of St Mellons Golf and Country Club and generally adopted:

1. Players are asked to collect bomb and shell splinters from the fairways to save these causing damage to the mowers.
2. In competitions, during gunfire or while bombs are falling, players may take cover without penalty for ceasing play.
3. The positions of known delayed-action bombs are marked by red and white flags placed at reasonably, but not guaranteed, safe distances from the bombs.
4. Shell and/or bomb splinters on the greens may be removed without penalty. On the fairways or in bunkers within a club's length of a ball they may be moved without penalty and no penalty shall be incurred if a ball is thereby caused to move accidentally.
5. A ball moved by enemy action may be replaced as near as possible to where it lay, or if lost or destroyed a ball may be dropped not nearer the hole without penalty.
6. A ball lying in any crater may be lifted and dropped not nearer the hole preserving the line to the hole, without penalty.
7. A player whose stroke is affected by the simultaneous explosion of a bomb or shell, or by machine-gun fire, may play another ball from the same place. Penalty one stroke.

One night during the Second World War a bomb fell on the course of a London Club but did not explode. One of the Members, who was a bomb expert, received a call in the middle of the night and was asked if he could defuse it. He left the comfort of his bed, and at considerable risk to himself, disarmed the bomb. In the morning mail, the following day, he received a letter from the Club Secretary informing him that his subscription was overdue.

45

Ben Hogan drives watched by his partner Sam Snead, in the 1953 Canada Cup (now the World Cup) at Wentworth.

The 'teeing ground' is the starting place for the hole to be played. It is a rectangular area two club-lengths in depth, the front and sides of which are defined by the outside limits of two tee-markers. A ball is outside the teeing ground when all of it lies outside the teeing ground. (Definition)

Henry Cotton won the first of three Open Championships in 1934 at Royal St George's Golf Club. His second round 65 not only helped him win by five shots, but it was the inspiration for the name of the famous Dunlop 65 golf ball.

Left Henry Cotton in 1934 with the Open Trophy.

Below Henry Cotton plays in front of huge crowds at Royal St George's during the 1934 Open Championship.

Bobby Locke's victory in the 1949 Open at Royal St George's will be forever remembered for an incident involving Harry Bradshaw who tied with Locke after 72 holes. Bradshaw had started his second round 4, 4, 4, 4 but at the 451 yard 5th hole he drove and found his ball lying inside a half broken bottle. Eye witnesses claim that the bottle was lying on its side and the ball ran along the ground into the bottle and tipped it upright.

The problem was, what to do? The Rules at that time were not clear on the distinction between 'movable' and 'immovable' obstructions and there was some doubt as to whether the ball was unplayable given that Bradshaw might have been able to 'dislodge it into a playable position'. Today, of course, the Rules are clear and Bradshaw would have been in no doubt that he could obtain free relief from the bottle (Rule 24-1). Bradshaw, a delightfully quick player, decided to play the ball, perhaps because he believed in the basic principle that a 'ball shall be played as it lies'. Understandably a little upset by the incident, he scored 6 at the hole and although he tied with Bobby Locke after 4 rounds, Locke won the play-off with rounds of 67 and 68.

Left Roberto de Vincenzo.

It would seem that every golfer in the entire world was watching television to see the fateful closing stages of the 1968 Masters.

Roberto de Vicenzo, the reigning Open Champion, took the lead in the final round reaching the turn in 31 strokes. A dropped shot at the 18th was the only blemish in the round and a 65 looked as if it would be good enough to win.

Bob Goalby was also having a splendid round and with a par at the 18th the tournament was tied. The play-off, over 18 holes, would take place the next day.

Then disaster struck. On checking de Vicenzo's card it was noticed that a 4, and not a 3, had been recorded at the 17th hole and his score added up to 66 and not 65.

The ruling was very clear. On completion of the round the marker shall sign the card and hand it to the competitor. The competitor shall check his score for each hole, settle any doubtful points with the Committee, ensure that the marker has signed the card, countersign the card himself and return it to the Committee as soon as possible. The *competitor* is solely responsible for the correctness of the score recorded for each hole. The Committee is responsible for the addition of scores.

If a score had been recorded lower than actually taken de Vicenzo would have been disqualified. As the recorded score was higher than actually taken the score stood as 66. De Vicenzo was stuck with the higher score and nothing could be done. He was now in second place.

Sometimes the Rules can be cruel but golf is a game of self discipline and no better example highlights this principle than this case.

Below Peter Thomson five times winner of the Open Championship, with fellow-competitors Frank Phillips and Kel Nagle the winner of the Centennial Open in 1960.

Right Jack Nicklaus and Arnold Palmer enjoy a light-hearted moment.

One of the stranger events in Jack Nicklaus's career was the story he relates of the play-off, with Arnold Palmer, for the 1962 US Open when he led by two strokes standing on the 18th tee.

On the 18th green Nicklaus putted up to about 18 inches, marked the position of his ball and lifted it. Palmer, who was at the back of the green in three, no doubt felt that his only chance was to hole his next shot. The ball ran past the hole and he casually backhanded the short putt but missed. He picked up his ball and the coin of Nicklaus, conceding defeat.

Joe Dey, the USGA official in charge of the game, intervened and stated that Nicklaus must hole out to have a score to win the tournament. Nicklaus duly replaced his ball and holed the putt, winning in 71 to an accredited 74 by Palmer.

Joe Dey was absolutely correct at that time and it was to be almost 30 years before the interpretation of the Rule regarding a stroke play play-off was changed. Today, if one competitor concedes defeat it is not necessary for the other to complete the play-off hole or holes to be declared the winner. (Decision 33-6/3)

50

Opposite Jack Nicklaus birdies the penultimate hole on the way to winning the 1986 Masters, his eighteenth 'major'.

Arnold Palmer writes:
'On the occasion of the Centenary of the Rules of Golf Committee of the Royal and Ancient Golf Club, I am reminded of an incident that occurred the year that I won my first Open Championship, at Royal Birkdale. (1961)

'In the second round, the winds were ferocious and the scores were accordingly high. I put my ball in a sand bunker at the 16th hole, took my stance and, before I could complete the shot, the wind moved the ball ... not quite an inch but still it moved the ball. I asked for a ruling on the spot. I was told by an official that there was no penalty to be assessed. However, when I finished the round with a 72 and was tied with Dai Rees, I was told that the Committee wanted to talk to me before I signed my card. I was then informed that I had incurred a one-stroke penalty and I posted a 73 instead of a 72, leaving me a stroke behind Dai. As things turned out, I won by a stroke over Dai the next day.'

A player has 'addressed the ball' when he has taken his stance and has grounded his club, except that in a hazard a player has addressed the ball when he has taken his stance. (Definition)

If a player's ball in play moves after he has addressed it (other than as a result of a stroke), the player shall be deemed to have moved the ball and shall incur a penalty of one stroke. The player shall replace the ball unless the movement occurs after he has begun his swing and he does not discontinue his swing. (Rule 18-2b)

53

Left Arnold Palmer acknowledges his 'army' of fans at the 1995 Open Championship at St Andrews.

Gary Player, already twice winner of the Open Championship, led the 1974 Open at Royal Lytham & St Annes from the start. However, at the penultimate hole his second shot disappeared into long grass at the edge of the green and the five minutes of permitted search time ticked away. With only seconds left the ball was found. But there was to be more drama on the last. His second shot ran over the green, coming to rest close to the Clubhouse. He had to play his ball onto the green left-handed with the back of his putter. He managed to do so and went on to win his third Open Championship.

Right Gary Player with the Open trophy having won the 1968 Championship.

Far Right Gary Player and his caddie 'Rabbit'. Player used to say 'The more I practise, the luckier I get.'

Below Lee Trevino at impact.

Below right Tony Jacklin at Royal Lytham & St Annes, on his way to winning the 1969 Open Championship.

Right Tom Watson birdies the 18th hole to win the 1977 Open Championship at Turnberry.

Below Jack Nicklaus congratulates Watson after their epic 'duel in the sun'.

The fact that the Ailsa Course, Turnberry, has staged three Open Championships is, in itself, remarkable. In 1942 three aircraft runways were constructed, and hangers, stores and administrative offices were built on the links land. Fortunately, the post-War government was persuaded to finance the design and restoration of the Course and the Ailsa Course was re-opened in 1951.

During the latter part of the Second World War some British POWs were in a camp in Germany when one of them received a hickory-shafted niblick in a Red Cross parcel. After hitting a few stones and the like about the camp the POWs began to make alternative balls. Everything was going along fine until one day the 'escape' officer whispered to one of the POWs that tomorrow was the day for the escape. 'I can't do that,' came the immediate response. 'Have you not heard – I will be playing golf!'

Left Seve Ballesteros chips to within inches of the hole to win the 1988 Open at Royal Lytham and St Annes.

Nine years earlier at Royal Lytham the result was the same, but Ballesteros's play was somewhat different. In his final round he hit only two fairways, but his short game got him round in 70 for a three stroke victory. His recovery shots included one on the 16th hole from a part of the Course which was being used as a car park for the week.

A car is an 'obstruction' and if it is readily movable it should be treated as a movable obstruction. Otherwise, it would be an immovable obstruction. (Decision 24/8)

Below Seve Ballesteros plays from under a tree in the 1996 Irish Open.

Left Greg Norman with his caddie at the Orchard Club in Manila, Philippines.

Below Greg Norman acknowledges the crowd walking up the 18th hole at Royal St George's in the 1993 Open.

Three days earlier, in the first round, Norman stood on the 13th tee one over par and his group was warned for slow play. Norman and the other members of his group Gary Evans and Tom Purtzer were advised that they were going to be individually timed. The effect was dramatic, the pace quickened and Norman made five consecutive birdies. With a par at the last, Norman came back in 31 and finished with 66.

For the purpose of preventing slow play, the Committee may, in the conditions of a competition (Rule 33-1), lay down pace of play guidelines including maximum periods of time allowed to complete a stipulated round, a hole or a stroke. (Note 2 to Rule 6-7)

Above Greg Norman and Nick Price – golfing rivals, but the best of friends.

Right Nick Price at the 1995 US Open at Shinnecock Hills.

Opposite Nick Faldo contemplates his second shot to the par 5 13th hole at Augusta during the final round of the 1996 Masters.

The player may have only one 'caddie' at any one time, under penalty of disqualification. For any breach of a Rule by his caddie, the player incurs the applicable penalty. (Rule 6-4)

Below Nick Price drives from the 9th tee of the Ailsa Course, Turnberry, on his way to winning the 1994 Open.

Above Laura Davies escapes in a shower of pine needles from underneath the pines at Bethesda Country Club, Washington DC.

Even the best players find themselves with unplayable lies now and then. In 1852 the applicable Rule stated:

'When a ball lies in a hole or in any place that the player considers it not playable, he shall, with the consent of his adversary, lift the ball, drop it in the hazard, and lose a stroke.

Should the adversary say, however, that he thinks the ball playable, then he (the adversary) plays the ball; if he makes the ball playable in two strokes, the two strokes count as if the player had played the ball; the player then plays the ball as if he had played it out; but if the adversary does not get the ball out at two strokes, then, as stated above, it is lifted and dropped, a stroke being lost.'

Right Jo Anne Carner, affectionately known as 'Big Moma'.

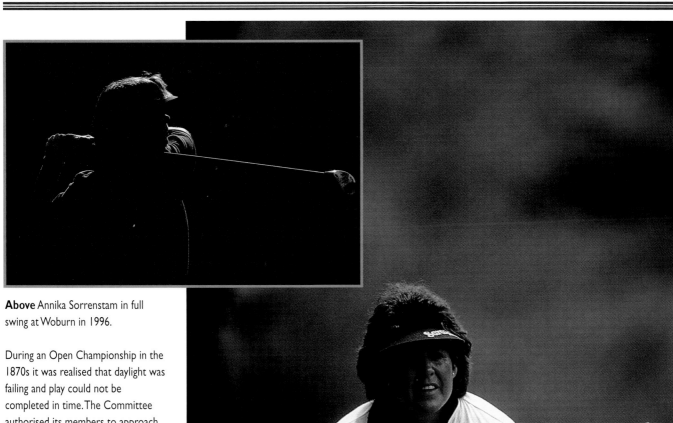

Above Annika Sorrenstam in full swing at Woburn in 1996.

During an Open Championship in the 1870s it was realised that daylight was failing and play could not be completed in time. The Committee authorised its members to approach players and enquire how they were doing. If they were not in contention the member could offer the player 'silver' as an inducement to discontinue play. The policy seemed to work well and might have been called 'disappearance money!'

Right Nancy Lopez watches anxiously.

Above From LA to LPGA? A young American girl on her way to play golf in Los Angeles.

Left Like father, like son. Young master Faldo demonstrates a keen eye for the ball.

Far left A future star, aged 2¹/₂.

Golf, like all sports, must nurture its roots and encourage youngsters of all ages and abilities to play and enjoy golf.

Opposite Lotte Neumann tees off at Palm Springs.

Right Greg Norman on his Harley Davidson in Singapore.

Below Colin Montgomerie and Ernie Els on the flight deck of a Boeing 737 at Manila airport.

Laddie Lucas, was born in the clubhouse of Prince's Golf Club, Sandwich and later became a Walker Cup golfer. During the Second World War he was a distinguished fighter pilot in the Royal Air Force. He writes:

'Coming out of France one day with the Wing, I happened to see two doubtful-looking aircraft at seven o'clock, up in the sun, 5000 feet above. "Watch them", I said to my No 3, "I don't fancy the look of them." We were high up.

'"It's OK, Wing Co", he retorted, "they're both ours".

'Forty seconds later a volley of cannon shells drilled into my Spitfire. It sounded as if I'd been hit by a London bus. Halfway back across the Straits, my engine called it a day. The options were obvious – not all pleasant.

'Then suddenly through the haze, away to the North, past Deal and St George's, I could see the faint outline of Prince's Clubhouse, It's prophetic, I thought, I'll try and stretch the glide, dead stick, and put down on the old, flat 1st fairway just past my nursery window.

'True to all known form, I missed the 1st fairway, the 2nd, the 6th and the 8th and finished up, out of bounds, in the marsh at the back of the old 9th green.

HOW WOULD YOU RULE?

Are the balls 'lost' if players search for a few moments and then remember that they have forgotten to drive?

Left Seve Ballesteros on his bike in the hills behind his home in Pedrena in Northern Spain.

Below Robert Allenby on a jet ski in Melbourne, Australia.

All competitors in a group must be present and ready to play at the time laid down by the Committee. The order of play is not relevant. (Decision 6-3a/2)

It doesn't matter who you are or how you get there, but you must get to the 1st tee on time. (Rule 6-3a)

WEATHER

BAD WEATHER IS NOT OF ITSELF
A GOOD REASON FOR DISCONTINUING PLAY.

I DIDN'T REALLY GET WET', is said by many golfers who, having played, come in absolutely soaked.

Fortunately golf is a game which is not dependent on good weather. It can be played in most kinds of weather but if the course becomes flooded, frozen, covered in snow, or it is too windy, play may have to be suspended by the Committee. Players in a match may discontinue play by agreement. In stroke play, the one occasion in which the player may discontinue play immediately, without first referring to the Committee, is if he believes there is danger from lightning. (Rule 6-8a)

Most golfers probably prefer to play in 'fair-weather' but the majority might just accept things the way they are. One thing is certain – you cannot fight the weather.

In certain parts of the world a *bomoh*, (a local witch doctor) is employed to keep the rain away. Such was the case in a tournament in Indonesia where the *bomoh* was told the dates of the event and that the fourth round should finish about 4.00pm. There was no rain for all four days and the event finished as planned, at 4.00pm. However, there was a tie which was to be decided by a sudden death play-off over holes one, eight and nine.

The pair tied for first place drove off at the 1st hole, and at the same moment the heavens opened. Everyone got soaked and the *bomoh* was asked for an explanation.

'What's this thing you call a "play-off" – I was told there were only four rounds'.

67

Above Greg Norman plays a bunker shot into the wind.

Opposite Michael Campbell is sheltered by his caddie as he takes a practice swing in the 1995 British Masters at Collingtree Park.

In making a 'stroke', a player shall not accept physical assistance or protection from the elements. (Rule 14-2). However, a player may hold an umbrella over his own head with one hand while gripping the club and playing with the other hand. (Decision 14-2/2)

HOW WOULD YOU RULE?

Two ladies were all square playing the last hole. One of them holed in 6 and the other was left with two putts from 8ft to win the match. At this point the heavens opened, the green became flooded and they agreed to discontinue the match and finish it the next day. (See Exception to Rule 6-8a). When they returned the following day they found that the greenkeeper had moved the hole. Instead of having two putts for the match from 8ft her ball was now lying 25 yds from the hole.

68

Wind is not an 'outside agency'. (Definition)

Above Craig Stadler loses his hat during the 1995 Irish Open at Mount Juliet Golf Club.

A player's hat is part of his 'equipment' and if the wind was to blow it onto his ball and move it, the player incurs a penalty stroke under Rule 18-2a and the ball must be replaced. (Decision 18-2a/17)

Left Seve Ballesteros in full flight into the wind during the 1988 Open at Royal Lytham & St Annes.

A player may not lay his golf bag parallel to the line of putt to shield the line from the wind. (Decision 1-2/2) Under Rule 1-2 no player or caddie shall take any action to influence the position or the movement of a ball, except in accordance with the Rules.

Right Nick Price contemplates his next shot on a windy day at St Andrews.

The Old Course, St Andrews has seven double greens and to avoid any confusion over which holes are which, white flags are used on the first nine holes and red flags are used on the second nine.

Realising that it was permissible, under the Rules, to have red flags on the front nine and yellow flags on the back nine a Club Secretary ordered 18 flags, half red and half yellow – and that's what he got!

Below Storm damage at Wentworth 1987.

A tree which has fallen to the ground due to a windstorm and is still attached to the stump is not 'ground under repair'. However, it is a matter for the Committee to examine all such storm damaged areas and decide if they should be declared 'ground under repair'. (Decision 25/9)

Top Left Jose Maria Olazabal wears a knitted hat to protect against the cold.

Left Greg Norman feeling the cold in St Andrews.

Some say that the East wind in St Andrews is so cold that it doesn't matter which direction it comes from!

Top right Seve Ballesteros in the fog.

Bad light may be a good reason to discontinue play. If the player discontinues play without specific permission from the Committee, he shall report to the Committee as soon as practicable. If he does so and the reason is satisfactory, the player incurs no penalty. Otherwise, the player shall be disqualified. (Rule 6-8a)

Right Florence Descampe wears a pair of large mittens to keep her hands warm.

Alternatively, a player may use a device to warm his or her hands during a round. (Decision 14-3/13)

Left A hail storm stops play at the 1993 Catalan Open.

Snow and natural ice, other than frost, are either 'casual water' or 'loose impediments', at the option of the player. (Definition)

Back in 1900 the Rules were a little different:

> When snow or ice lies on the putting greens, partners are recommended to make their own arrangements as to its removal or not, before commencing the match.

Below Winter golf in St Morritz, Switzerland.

Above Heavy rain causes a suspension of play during the 1995 Cannes Open at Royal Mougins Golf Club.

If all the area around the hole contains casual water, in stroke play the course should be considered unplayable and the Committee should suspend play under Rule 33-2d. In match play, the Committee should relocate the hole. (Decision 33-2d/2)

A round should only be cancelled where it would be grossly unfair not to cancel it. (Decision 33-2d/1)

Inset left A 'water hog' at work during the 1988 Open at Royal Lytham and St Annes.

Inset right Steve Richardson and caddie shelter under an umbrella at Sunningdale during the 1992 European Open.

Below Seve Ballesteros retrieves his ball from casual water.

'Casual water' is any temporary accumulation of water on the course, which is visible either before or after the player takes his stance and is not in a water hazard. (Definition)

A player is not obliged to use unreasonable effort to retrieve a ball from casual water. However, if it would not take unreasonable effort to retrieve a ball in casual water, the player must retrieve it. (Decision 25-1/1)

Above Deserted grandstands after a storm during the 1985 Open Championship at Royal St George's.

Right inset A 'weather warning' at the US Open. The clear blue skies give a false impression – an electrical storm is in the area.

Right Jack Nicklaus and Tom Watson shelter from a passing electrical storm on rocks during the 1977 Open at Turnberry.

Regrettably there have been fatalities and injuries from lightning on golf courses. Accordingly, certain provisions have been made in the Rules of Golf.

Rule 6-8a authorises a player to discontinue play if he considers that there is danger from lightning. This is one of the rare occasions when the player is virtually the final judge. The safety of players is paramount, especially as there is a common natural fear of lightning. (Decision 6-8b/5)

In addition, the Note under Rule 6-8b authorises the Committee to introduce a condition of competition that in potentially dangerous situations, such as lightning, all players must discontinue play immediately following a suspension of play by the Committee. Ordinarily, those in the process of playing a hole may complete that hole should they so wish. The intent of the condition is to enable the course to be cleared of players and spectators alike, as quickly as possible, when a potentially dangerous situation exists. (Decision 6-8b/7)

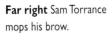

Above Ian Woosnam
drinking water to combat the
heat.

Right Sven Struver shows
how hot it can get.

Far right Sam Torrance
mops his brow.

When playing in the heat of the
day it is important to avoid
becoming dehydrated. A player is
entitled to pick up refreshment
during his rounds and find shade
when he can, but he must not
unduly delay play (Rule 6-7) or
discontinue play (Rule 6-8).

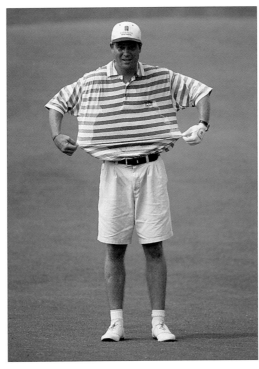

Right Craig Parry shelters from the heat of the sun in Indonesia.

A player may employ both a caddie and a second person to carry his umbrella and hold it over his head (except when a stroke is being made) to protect him from the sun. An umbrella carrier is an 'outside agency' and not a second caddie. (Decision 6-4/5)

Below A Rules official calls for assistance to fight a gorse fire at the 1989 Open at Royal Troon. A Rules official has many duties during a tournament. This may be one of the rare occasions when play is temporarily suspended for some players (eg danger or poor visibility) but not for the entire field.

Prior to any major event the wise Rules official spends a good deal of time trying to imagine all the likely problems which might arise so that he or she will be well prepared. Even for the most experienced official something strange may happen which could not be anticipated and such a case occurred at Royal Lytham and St Annes during the 1996 Open Championship.

Elizabeth Earnshaw, one of the first ladies to officiate at the Open, was accompanying the game with Brian Barnes during the first round. At the 15th hole he hooked his second shot into the grandstand beside the green. A Local Rule provided that in such circumstances if relief is required the player must drop a ball in the dropping zone nearest to which his ball originally lay, without penalty.

What could not be foreseen was that there was a man, with a broken leg, lying in the dropping zone. The medical team were on their way but had not arrived.

When Barnes arrived at the grandstand to find the man lying in the dropping zone, he took a new ball from his bag, signed it and gave it to him. As the Rules permit a player to stand outside a dropping zone when a ball is being dropped, Barnes felt there was just enough room in the zone for him to drop a ball. With the injured man's consent he did this and, under the circumstances, played an admirable chip on to the green.

All of this had been done to the obvious delight of the crowd who had been silently watching the proceedings unfold.

GREENS

W hat's the line? His caddie thought for a moment and replied with certainty: 'Slightly straight'.

It could be said that golf is made up of two games. (1) From tee to the green, and (2) Putting. Over the past century we have seen an enormous improvement in the standard of putting surface which may be the single most important reason for the lowering of scores. In 1744, Rule 1 stated 'You must Tee your Ball within a Club length of the Hole' (for the next drive). A very simple and straightforward Rule but imagine what the putting surface was like! In those days there was no lining, just a hole in the ground. Today we expect a perfect surface every time we play, forgetting that we are supposed to have some skill to overcome any imperfections.

Spike marks and the prohibition against their repair is a recurring topic of discussion amongst golfers. It has been argued that a player should be allowed to repair spike marks as such damage can make the skilled art of putting a lottery. The Rules of Golf Committees of the R&A and the USGA have consistently resisted such a change on the basis that it was never envisaged that golf would be played in perfect conditions and a golfer must adapt to the conditions which confront him.

The reasoning is that damage created by spike marks cannot be distinguished from damage or irregularities of surface caused by other things, and so to allow the repair of spike marks would entail permitting any damage or irregularity of surface on the putting green to be repaired. Such a deviation from the general principles of the game is considered unacceptable.

In addition, the increase of 'slow play' which would be a result of players attempting to perfect their line on every putt is a major consideration in any debate on this topic.

The location of the 'pins' is an important part in the setting up of a course and despite what has been written about this subject it all comes down to common sense. A club mixed-foursomes competition is not the third round of an Open Championship and the pins should be set accordingly.

Opposite Ben Crenshaw's ball comes to rest overhanging the hole.

When any part of the ball overhangs the lip of the hole, the player is allowed enough time to reach the hole without unreasonable delay and an additional ten seconds to determine whether the ball is at rest. (Rule 16-2)

Above The 2nd and 16th holes on the Old Course, St Andrews, share one of seven double greens.

The 'putting green' is all ground of the hole being played which is specially prepared for putting or otherwise defined as such by the Committee. A ball is on the putting green when any part of it touches the putting green. (Definition)

A player must not play a ball which lies on a 'wrong putting green'. (Rule 25-3) That part of a double green serving the other hole is not a 'wrong putting green' unless the Committee divides the green by use of stakes or a line. (Decision 25-3/1)

Right Tom Lehman surveys his putt on the 1st green at Oak Hill during the 1995 Ryder Cup Matches.

Left Members of the greens staff assist with ball mark repairs at the Blue Canyon Country Club in Thailand.

Below Jack Nicklaus replaces his ball on the putting green.

A ball on the putting green may be lifted and, if desired, cleaned. A ball so lifted shall be replaced on the spot from which it was lifted. (Rule 16-1b) The position of the ball shall be marked before it is lifted under a Rule which requires it to be replaced. (Rule 20-1)

The Note to Rule 20 states, in part, that the position of a ball to be lifted should be marked by placing a ball-marker, a small coin or other similar object immediately behind the ball.

When the word 'should' is used in the Rules it is a recommendation and in this instance the intention is to emphasise the best way to mark a ball. Provided the ball is replaced on the same spot from which it was lifted the requirement of the Rule is satisfied.

A player may repair an old hole plug or ball mark, whether or not the player's ball lies on the putting green. Any other damage to the putting green shall not be repaired if it might assist the player in his subsequent play of the hole. (Rule 16-1c)

Main picture Putting amidst a minefield of spike marks left by previous players.

Inset Vijay Singh repairs a ball mark on the green.

A player is not only permitted to repair ball marks on the putting green, as a matter of good etiquette, he is encouraged to do so. (Rule 16-1c)

80

The 'Himalayas' putting green at St Andrews.

The Ladies Putting Club was formed in 1867 and is the oldest ladies golf club in the world. The Course, which adjoins the second fairway of the Old Course, is known as the Himalayas because of its hummocky lay out.

    The Rules of the Green include permission to strike the pin with the first putt on a hole, but not thereafter.

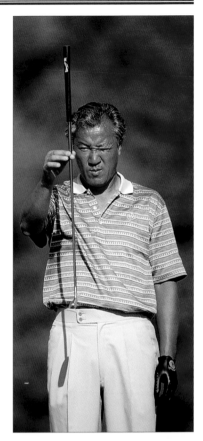

Above Joakim Haegmann 'down on all fours' to read the line of his putt.

The 'line of putt' is the line which the player wishes his ball to take after a stroke on the putting green. (Definition)

Right and Far right Curtis Strange and Isao Aoki plumb bobbing.

A player may use his putter as a plumb-line to assist him in determining the slope on a putting green. (Decision 14-3/12) However, he may not use a weight suspended by a piece of string for the same purpose. This is an artificial device, and its use would result in disqualification. (Decision 14-3/11)

Right Putting through shadow.

A player's caddie may not cast his shadow on the putting green for the purpose of indicating to the player a line for putting. (Decision 8-2b/1)

Opposite The first players of the day putt through the early morning dew at St Mellion, Cornwall.

Dew and frost are not loose impediments (Definition). The removal of dew or frost from the player's line of play is not permitted. Such action is deemed to improve the line of play and is in breach of Rule 13-2 or, on the putting green Rule 16-1a, unless it occurs incidentally to some other action permitted under the Rules, e.g. removing loose impediments, repairing ball marks on the putting green. (Decision 13-2/35)

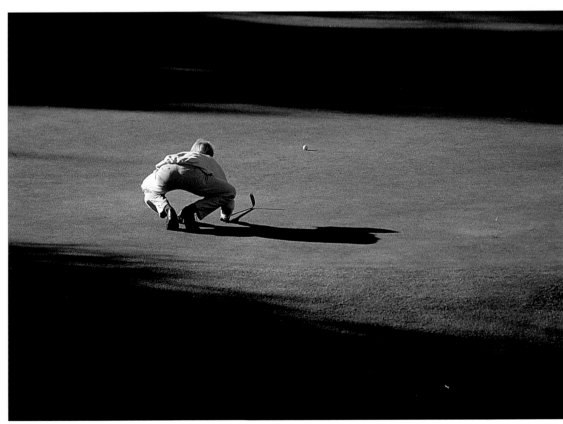

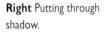

Top left and right A putting method adopted by Bernhard Langer.

Bottom left Sam Snead using a permitted 'side saddle' putting style. In the 1960s Sam Snead putted 'croquet' style with great success, until standing astride the line of putt was prohibited by a new Rule introduced in 1968.

The player shall not make a stroke on the putting green from a stance astride, or with either foot touching, the line of putt or an extension of that line behind the ball. (Rule 16-1e)

Bottom right Patty Sheehan celebrates another victory on the LPGA Tour. She is not testing the surface of the green (Rule 16-1d) or adopting a radical solution to the spike mark problem!

Three of the game's great putters

Above left Bob Charles; **Above middle** Phil Mickelson; **Above right** Bobby Locke

Bobby Locke's victory in the 1957 Open at St Andrews was marked by an unusual incident on the last green. Locke replaced his ball incorrectly before holing a 2-foot putt for victory by three shots. The Committee considered the facts and it was decided that as Locke had gained no possible advantage through this 'technical error' no action be taken. The decision was based on 'equity and the spirit of the game'. Locke, whose plus fours were his trademark, wished a daily reminder of the Committee's compassion and never wore plus fours again.

Left Some players manage to hole out without using their putters.

Four years had passed since the last 'hole-in-one' in the US Open and within an hour and a half in the second round of the 1989 Championship, four players completed the feat at the 6th hole at Oak Hill Country Club. In the first group, Doug Weaver holed with a 7-iron followed shortly afterwards by Mark Wiebe, then Jerry Pate and later Nick Price, all using a 7-iron.

The USGA's P J Boatwright, who had set the pin positions for the day, was asked how difficult the second round position was. 'Obviously very easy' he replied.

LIES

THE BALL NEVER LIES AS WELL AS THE GOLFER.

'THE BALL SHALL BE PLAYED as it lies' is not one of the original thirteen Rules but it is a long established principle of the game.

Golf is a game with an element of chance and one must accept the rough with the smooth. It is part of the challenge of the game to overcome the unevenness of stance and the variations in the lie. It might be easier to forever play the ball off a tee but in the end it would probably be a bore. There is a huge variation of courses, from the desert to the tropical and the player must be prepared to adapt his game.

Adverse conditions, including the poor condition of the course or the existence of mud, are sometimes so general, particularly during winter months, (or summer months, depending where you live), that the Committee may decide to grant relief by a temporary Local Rule either to protect the course or to promote fair and pleasant play.

The Local Rule might read as follows:
A ball lying on any 'closely mown area' through the green may, without penalty, be moved or be lifted, cleaned and placed within six inches of where it originally lay, but not nearer the hole. After the ball has been so moved or placed, it is in play.

It may be wise to mark the position of the ball, for reference purposes, before lifting it, but it must not be a requirement of the Local Rule because the ball is not being replaced. (See Rule 20-1)

Opposite Mark Roe beside the 3rd fairway at the Emirates Club in Dubai doesn't have much of a shot, even with a club in his hands.

HOW WOULD YOU RULE?

If a player's ball comes to rest inside the clubhouse, which is not out of bounds, is he permitted to open a door or window in order to play out?

Above Seve Ballesteros and the crowd at Woburn see the funny side.

Right Seve Ballesteros receives a ruling from Chief Referee John Paramor on the final hole of the 1994 Volvo Masters at Valderrama, Spain.

The doubtful point was whether or not a hole and associated damage at the base of a tree, close to the player's ball, had been made by a burrowing animal. If so, even though the player's only reasonable stroke was a sideways stroke onto the fairway, he would have been entitled to relief without penalty, under Rule 25-1b. (Decision 25-1b/22)

In the absence of any evidence that the hole had been caused by a burrowing animal, free relief was denied.

A burrow is a hole or tunnel in the ground made by certain animals, such as rabbits, moles, ground hogs and gophers, for shelter and habitation. Thus, a burrowing animal is an animal that makes a hole in which it may live. Since a dog does not dig holes for habitation or shelter, a hole made by a dog is not a burrowing animal hole. (Decision 25/19)

The Referee's decision is final. (Rule 34-2)

Above Seve Ballesteros plays
a miraculous recovery shot,
under a tree, over a
swimming pool wall and
nearly on to the green – from
where he holed his pitch for a
birdie on the 72nd hole of the
1993 European Masters at
Crans Montana, Switzerland.

Left Tommy Nakajima tangles
with the Muirfield rough
during the 1992 Open
Championship.

Right Sandy Lyle plays out of the trees at Crans-sur-Sierre in Switzerland.

A player must not improve his lie, the area of his intended swing or his line of play, but he is entitled to 'fairly take his stance'. (Rule 13-2)

The use of the word 'fairly' is intended to limit the player to what is reasonably necessary to take a stance without unduly improving his lie, area of intended swing or line of play. He must accommodate the situation in which the ball is found and take a stance as normal as the circumstances permit. What is 'fair' must be determined in the light of all the circumstances. (Decision 13-2/1)

Below Nick Faldo up a tree at the San Roque Club in Spain.

The player is the sole judge as to whether his ball is unplayable. (Rule 28)

Above Jose Maria Olazabal plays from beside a tree during the 1991 Ryder Cup at Kiawah Island.

A player may stand on one leg to play a shot or lean against a tree to do so provided the ball is fairly struck. (Rule 14-1)

Left Ian Woosnam plays left-handed from the 'bush' in Australia.

A player may play a left-handed stroke with any part of the clubhead, provided the ball is fairly struck. (Rule 14-1 and Decision 14-1/1)

'The fairway is that part of the course where the game is meant to be played'. (Anon)

Above and right Tom Lehman escapes from a bush on the 6th hole during the final round of the 1996 Open at Royal Lytham and St Annes.

Tom Lehman, 1996 Open Champion, recounts an occasion where the Rules saved him some shots.

'I was playing in the minitours in 1988 and many hazards and GURs were not marked or lined at all. I hit an approach shot on the 17th hole into the rocks bordering the pond adjacent to the green. Not only was it in the rocks, but it was in the edge of a burrowing animal hole. My partner said I was in the water hazard. I felt I wasn't and was entitled to relief from the hole. Rocks like that were normally lined as part of the hazard, but since this wasn't marked at all, the Rule was in my favour. The actual line of the hazard is the edge of the water and vertically upward. Since I was outside of that line, I was entitled to relief and got up and down for par, saving one or two shots.'

It is a Committee responsibility to define accurately the margins of water hazards (Rule 33-2a). Also, it is a long established principle, in the spirit of the game, that in the vast majority of cases any doubt should be resolved in the favour of the player.

Left Rosie Jones searches for her ball during the 1996 Solheim Cup at St Pierre, Wales. A golf ball can finish in some funny places but seldom to the amusement of the player who hit it there.

In searching for his ball anywhere on the course, the player may touch or bend long grass, bushes or the like, but only to the extent necessary to find and identify it, provided that this does not improve the lie of the ball, the area of his intended swing or the line of his play. (Rule 12-1)

Left Divots on the practice ground.

Below Ian Woosnam takes a large divot from the 18th fairway at Blue Canyon Country Club, Phuket, Thailand.

In the best interests of others it is a matter of good etiquette to repair divots. This may be done by replacing the cut turf or filling the hole with a mixture of soil and seed.

A club in the South of England decided to have a purge on the general upkeep of the course and the Secretary put a notice on the board as follows:

'Members are asked to replace all divits'.

Within hours about fifty of his members phoned him to say that he did not know how to spell. This did not seem to upset the Secretary because he said that it was fifty more members than normally read his notices!

Top left Larry Mize deep in the rough in Jamaica.

Top right T. C. Chen has a double hit when chipping out of thick rough. At the time he led the 1985 US Open at Oakland Hills by four shots with fifteen holes to play. The effect of the double hit was to turn a possible 5 into an 8 on a par-4 hole and in the end he finished second, one stroke behind Andy North.

If the player's club strikes the ball more than once in the course of a stroke, the player shall count the stroke and add a penalty stroke, making two strokes in all. (Rule 14-4)

Bottom left Ian Baker-Finch tangling with the deep rough in his home country Australia.

Bottom right A ball deep in Bermuda grass.

Above and left Rules officials examine
Corey Pavin's ball in the edge of the bunker
during the 1992 US Open at Pebble Beach.

It was ruled that the ball was in the bunker and
Pavin declared it unplayable. He dropped a ball, in
the bunker, keeping the point where the ball lay
directly between the hole and the spot on which
the ball was dropped under penalty of one stroke.
(Rule 28c and Decision 28/4)

*A 'bunker' is a hazard consisting of a prepared area of
ground, often a hollow, from which turf or soil has been
removed and replaced with sand or the like. Grass-
covered ground bordering or within a bunker is not part
of the bunker. The margin of a bunker extends vertically
downwards, but not upwards. A ball is in a bunker when
it lies in or any part of it touches the bunker.
(Definition)*

Left A spectator climbs a tree to help Padraig Harrington identify his ball during the 1996 Irish Open at Druids Glen.

Provided the player can identify his ball he does not have to retrieve it. (Decision 27/14)

It can sometimes be a source of amusement if someone climbs a tree to retrieve a player's ball. But the player may not find it very amusing if, in the process, the ball moves and the player has not made his intentions clear. To avoid any question being raised as to whether a penalty would be incurred under Rule 18-2a (Ball at Rest Moved) the player should make it clear that, if it is his ball, he will proceed under the unplayable ball Rule. The same would apply if the player wished to shake the tree to dislodge the ball (Decision 18-2a/27).

Opposite Ball embedded in cactus plant, Desert Mountain Golf Club, Arizona.

The ball may always be played as it lies. However, if the player elects to declare the ball unplayable he may, under penalty of one stroke, drop a ball within two club-lengths of the point on the ground immediately below the place where the ball lies in the cactus. (Rule 28b and Decision 28/11)

Left Jarmo Sandelin plays a miraculous shot against the wall behind the 17th green of the Old Course, St Andrews, to save his par during the 1995 Alfred Dunhill Cup.

A 'stroke' is the forward movement of the club made with the intention of fairly striking at and moving the ball. (Definition)

Below Tom Watson found himself in a similar position during the 1984 Open Championship.

Objects defining 'out of bounds' such as walls, fences, stakes and railings are not 'obstructions' (Definition) and the ball must be played as it lies or declared unplayable.

In order to strike the ball fairly, it must be swung at with the clubhead. If the ball is moved by any other method, it has been pushed, scraped or spooned in breach of Rule 14-1. (Decision 14-1/4)

Above Ernie Els cannot find his ball in amongst the azalea bushes on the 13th hole at Augusta during the final round of the 1994 Masters Tournament.

A ball is 'lost' if it is not found or identified as his by the player within five minutes after the player's side or his or their caddies have begun to search for it. (Definition)

Left Sheep grazing on the course at Royal North Devon.

Extract from the *Daily Telegraph* 3rd June 1995:
Golfer wins by a sheep at 17th hole.

A golfer had a stroke of luck after his drive from the 17th tee wedged beneath the tail of a grazing sheep.

Peter Croke chased the ewe as it ran off before conveniently depositing the ball 30 yards closer to the green, while John Maher watched in disbelief.

Mr Croke, a deputy headmaster, lined up to take his next shot as the animal walked off apparently unharmed. He went on to finish the 416-yard par-4 hole in 5 shots to win the match.

Officials at the Southerndown Golf Club, near Porthcawl, South Wales, later found the Rules had been observed because a footpath where the sheep finally dropped the ball was in bounds. The course runs across the common land, with golfers and grazing sheep normally oblivious to one another.

The drive, which should have soared skywards, hit the ewe 40 yards ahead.

Mr Croke, 47, of Cowbridge, South Glamorgan, said: 'The sheep looked mildly surprised by the whole thing, but we were in hysterics. It walked off towards the 17th hole and then seemed to shake the ball free like laying an egg.'

The following letter appeared in the *Daily Telegraph* on 7th June 1995:

One in hole

Sir – I cannot help wondering if the officials of the Club where the golf ball became wedged beneath a sheep's tail (report June 2) are trying to pull the wool over our eyes.

Under Rule 19-1a of the game, if a ball in motion after a stroke comes to rest in an animate outside agency (the sheep), the player shall drop the ball as near as possible to the spot where the sheep was when the ball came to rest in it. The ball may be cleaned.

Contrary to the report, the player did not proceed properly and his opponent could have claimed the hole. I feel a little sheepish about bringing this to your attention, but felt matters should be put right.
John Glover
Rules Secretary
Royal and Ancient Golf Club of St Andrews, Fife.

In the third round of a US Tour event in 1987, Craig Stadler unwittingly breached Rule 13-3 when he knelt on a towel to keep his trousers dry. This Rule states that a player is entitled to place his feet firmly in taking his stance, but he shall not build a stance.

Prior to the Stadler incident Decision 13-3/2 had been published stating that the act of kneeling on a towel, in such circumstances, was building a stance. The really unfortunate part of the incident was that the breach was only brought to the attention of the Committee during the final round of the competition by a TV viewer who thought he was watching live action. Because Stadler had returned a score card containing a score for a hole lower than actually taken he was disqualified (Rule 6-6d).

Above Craig Stadler returns to Torry Pines near San Diego in 1995 and takes his revenge. The tree was dying from a fungus and Stadler was only too pleased to assist in cutting it down. He also recreated his stroke for the assembled media.

Right Colin Montgomerie plays from a flower bed in front of the 10th green at the Belfry during the 1993 Ryder Cup.

A player is not entitled to free relief from a flower bed unless it has been declared 'ground under repair.'

Opposite Annika Sorrenstam amidst a sea of leaves during the 1994 Solheim Cup Matches at the Greenbrier.

'Loose impediments' are natural objects such as stones, leaves, twigs, branches and the like, dung, worms and insects and casts or heaps made by them, provided they are not fixed or growing, are not solidly embedded and do not adhere to the ball. (Definition)

HAZARDS

IT'S ALL VERY WELL TO PUNISH A BAD SHOT BUT THE RIGHT TO ETERNAL DAMNATION
SHOULD BE RESERVED FOR A HIGHER TRIBUNAL THAN A GREEN COMMITTEE.
Bernard Darwin after following seven straight pars with a sixteen.

GOLF IS A GAME played in a larger and more complex arena than probably any other sport. It is not played in an area of uniform dimensions, but on land which often reflects a particular country's climate, terrain, and vegetation. 'Water hazards' can be as large as oceans or small, like a stream, but equally treacherous for the golfer. Bunkers are the other type of hazard on a golf course and also vary greatly in size and shape. Hazards are the defence mechanism of a golf course and should provide challenge to the player without being purely penal.

Special Rules apply when a ball is in a hazard. *A player is prohibited from testing the condition of the hazard or similar hazard, he must not touch the ground in the hazard or water in the water hazard with a club or otherwise and loose impediments lying in or touching the hazard cannot be touched or moved. (Rule 13-4)*

Some years ago a player hit his ball on to the beach (a lateral water hazard) from the Nairn Golf Course, near Inverness. He played a splendid long shot off the beach which unfortunately crossed the fairway and his ball ended up amongst some gorse. He looked for five minutes but could not find the ball, so he returned to the place from where he had played the previous stroke and dropped a ball. After the passage of time the tide had come in and the ball was now lying in water. Each time he was about to address the ball the incoming tide lifted the ball and then dragged it out to sea. Moments later the tide would reverse the process and bring the ball back to its original position.

The player called for a Rules official to see what he was allowed to do. A Rules official may advise a player of his options under the Rules, but not the option he should take or the type of shot he should play – that would be advice (Rule 8).

The official explained the options of the Rules to do with a water hazard (Rule 26-2b) and a ball moving in water (Rule 14-6) and added, 'Whatever you are going to do for God's sake do it quickly'.

Whoever said that golf was meant to be 'fair'.

Opposite Costantino Rocca in the Road bunker during the four-hole play off for the 1995 Open Championship at St Andrews.

105

Gary Player extricates his ball from an awkward lie in a bunker at Royal Lytham & St Annes, but then falls into the bunker.

Even if Player had failed to get his ball out of the bunker, he would incur no penalty for touching the ground in the hazard as a result of falling, provided he does not test the condition of the hazard or improve the lie of the ball. (Exception 1 to Rule 13-4)

Gary Player writes:

'Thank goodness for the Royal and Ancient Golf Club of St Andrews and their contribution to this great game of golf. They have spent so much effort in so many different ways and above all, are continuously working on the Rules of Golf which are so important to us all to maintain a discipline which is the tradition since the game was founded.

I was playing in a tournament at Greensboro in the late '60s. We were playing 36 holes on the final day due to a rain out. After the third round, I checked my card thoroughly and forgot to sign it. I walked out of the scoring tent by 5 yards, remembered I hadn't signed it, walked back and signed it. I reported the incident to the PGA before I teed off in the final round. The answer was, "You are disqualified for leaving the tent."

The conclusion is that I hope people will realise the importance of spending time on your score card at the conclusion of a round. You spend 4 hours playing; it's worthwhile spending 5 minutes checking. There have been many suggestions that the Rule should be changed. I disagree. The responsibility rests with the golfer himself. This is the discipline that golf requires.'

Above Ball resting against rake in bunker.

It is recommended that rakes be placed outside bunkers, as far away from the bunkers as is practical and in positions where they will be least likely to affect play. (Decision Misc/2)

A rake is a 'movable obstruction' which may be removed anywhere on the course. If the ball moves, it must be replaced and there is no penalty provided that the movement of the ball is directly attributable to the removal of the obstruction. (Rule 24-1)

Left Greg Norman plays from the sand in Dubai.

If a player playing a shot in a bunker accidentally touches the sand when making his backswing he incurs a penalty of loss of hole in match play and two strokes in stroke play. (Rule 13-4b and Decision 13-4/31)

On courses accessible to the general public it has been known for children to play in the bunkers leaving footprints, holes and sandcastles. These are simply considered to be irregularities of surface from which relief, without penalty, is not available. (Decision 33-8/9)

109

HOW WOULD YOU RULE?

In stroke play, is there any difference in the penalty incurred if, through the green, a player plays two successive strokes with a wrong ball or two different wrong balls in succession?

Payne Stewart plays from the 8th fairway at Pebble Beach in California against the glorious backdrop of Carmel beach.

The Committee shall define accurately the margins of water hazards (Rule 33-2) – it is sometimes not possible to mark both sides!

In 1744 the Water Hazard Rule stated:

'If your ball comes among Watter or any Wattery filth, you are at liberty to take out your ball & bringing it behind the hazard and teeing it, you may play it with any club and allow your Adversary a Stroke for so getting your ball.'

In order to treat a ball as lost in a water hazard there must be reasonable evidence to that effect.

The term 'reasonable evidence' in Rule 26-1 is purposely and necessarily broad so as to permit sensible judgements to be reached on the basis of all the relevant circumstances of particular cases. A player may not deem his ball lost in a water hazard simply because he thinks the ball may be in the hazard. The evidence must be preponderantly in favour of its being in the hazard. Otherwise, the ball must be considered lost outside the hazard and the player must proceed under Rule 27-1. (Decision 26-1/1)

Right Bunkers are easier to get into than get out of.

Bernard Darwin writing of the bunkers in St Andrews 'Some were carved out of the dunes by sheep for shelter and others were just large enough for an angry man and his niblick!'

Below The bunkers at the Lake Nona Club in Florida contain sand and trees.

Grass-covered ground within a bunker is not part of the bunker. The same principle applies to a tree. The margin of a bunker does not extend vertically upwards. (Decision 13/2)

Fallen leaves are 'loose impediments' and, when a player's ball is in a bunker, they must not be touched or moved. (Rule 13-4c)

Above The fairway bunker at the 4th hole, Royal St George's.

Railway 'sleepers' are not an uncommon edging to a bunker (or a water hazard) and it is a matter for the Committee to decide whether they should be declared an integral part of the course. (Definition of 'Obstructions')

During the 1979 English Amateur Championship, Reg Gladding had finished all square in his quarter final match and went into tie holes. The first three were halved and then he drove his ball into the top of this bunker. Fearing an avalanche he carefully approached the ball from below and then gingerly took his stance. During the swing he lost his balance and fell backwards head over heels down to the bottom of the bunker. Sand came tumbling down after him together with his ball which struck him in the back. It is possible that he had broken a number of Rules but the sad conclusion was that because the ball had hit him he lost the hole and the match (Rule 19-2a).

Left The short 11th hole on the Old Course, St Andrews has deep bunkers in front of and to the left of the green.

A Committee may make a Local Rule clarifying that the face of a bunker which consists of stacked turf is neither (a) part of the bunker nor (b) a 'closely mown area' for the purpose of applying Rule 25-2, the embedded ball Rule. (Decision 33-8/39)

A man asked the Rules of Golf Committee if it is permissible to play stroke and distance (Unplayable Ball – Rule 28) when a ball is lying in a bunker.

He concluded by stating, 'Please answer "yes" or "no" as any more legal ruling only tends to confuse me'.

John Cook plays from the fairway bunker on the 8th hole at Augusta.

A ball is in a bunker when it lies in or any part of it touches the bunker. (Definition)

Right Seve Ballesteros attempts to play out of Rae's Creek which crosses in front of the 13th green at Augusta. On this occasion he failed. In total he has played three strokes and his ball still lies in the Creek. If he does not want to play the ball as it lies, under Rule 26-2a, Ballesteros has the following options, under penalty of one stroke.

1. He could drop a ball as near as possible to the spot from which he had played his last shot, and play from there – in which case he would be playing five from within the hazard; or

2. He could drop a ball behind the creek keeping the point at which the ball last crossed the margin directly between the hole and the spot on which he dropped the ball, and play from there, playing five; or

3. He could go back to where he played his second shot from and play from there as that is the spot from which he played his last stroke from outside the hazard. Again, he would be playing five.

Opposite Darren Clarke plays from within a water hazard during the 1994 Czech Open.

116 Ernie Els plays from within a lateral water hazard
on the 16th hole at Thana City in Bangkok, Thailand.

*A 'lateral water hazard' is a water hazard or any part of a water hazard so situated that it is
not possible or is deemed by the Committee to be impracticable to drop a ball behind the
water hazard in accordance with Rule 26-1b. A lateral water hazard should be defined by red
stakes or lines.*

*If a ball is in, or is lost in, a water hazard and the ball last crossed the margin of the hazard where
it is marked as a lateral hazard, the player has two additional options. He may, under penalty of
one stroke, drop a ball outside the hazard, within two club-lengths of and not nearer the hole than:*

1. The point where the original ball last crossed the margin of the hazard; or
2. A point on the opposite margin of the hazard equidistant from the hole. (Rule 26-1c)

Left Jack Nicklaus plays from the dropping zone on the 12th hole at Augusta having hit his tee shot into the water hazard.

When a Committee establishes a Dropping Zone (DZ) or Ball Drop the procedure for dropping and re-dropping is as follows:

(a) The player does not have to stand in the DZ when dropping the ball.

(b) The dropped ball must strike a part of the course within the DZ.

(c) If the DZ is defined by a white line, the line is within the DZ.

(d) The dropped ball does not have to come to rest within the DZ.

(e) The dropped ball must be re-dropped if it rolls into a hazard, onto a putting green, out of bounds, or more than two club-lengths from where it first struck a part of the course.

(f) The dropped ball may roll nearer the hole provided it comes to rest within two club-lengths of the spot where it first struck a part of the course within the DZ and not into any position covered by (e).

(g) Subject to the provisions of (e) and (f), the dropped ball may come to rest nearer the hole than its original position or estimated position. (Decision 33-8/34)

117

Below Colin Montgomerie appears to be walking on water as he leaves the 17th green at Druids Glen during the 1996 Irish Open.

Clubs & Balls

GOLF IS A CHALLENGE OF ONE'S TALENT AGAINST THE COURSE AND THE ELEMENTS
WITH A CLUB AND A BALL AND , IF APPLICABLE, A HANDICAP.
ARTIFICIAL DEVICES AND UNUSUAL EQUIPMENT ARE DEFINITELY NOT PERMITTED.

T HE MAIN CONTROLLING FACTOR of the game must surely be the ball. When the Rules of Golf Committee came on the scene the 'gutty' ball, even in its primitive stages, had ousted the 'feathery'. The gutty ball passed through many stages and had reached a state of perfection, with the best balls being sold at twelve shillings per dozen. The balls were economical in respect that the gutty could be melted and re-made and many professionals had their own moulds and made their own balls. Next came the rubber-core ball invented by Dr Haskell, of Cleveland, USA, and some of these were used in the Amateur Championship at Royal Liverpool, Hoylake in 1902. At that time they were not too well received because they were too lively on the putting green. However, they quickly improved and Alex Herd, in the same year used a rubber-core ball and won the Open Championship. The gutty ball was quickly superseded and in 1903 the use of the rubber-core ball became general. In 1920 John L. Low, then Chairman of the Rules of Golf Committee, feared the worst and prophesied 'Distance of hit, not quality of shot is to become the metier of the player'. That is certainly the attitude of many players today and some would 'kill' for another ten yards! There is no doubt that over the years the continued improvement of the ball, and its price, has been a main factor in the growth of the popularity of the game.

Golf, of course, is not only a matter of trying to hit the ball out of sight but perhaps, even more important, is a game of control.

Over the same period we have witnessed the tremendous improvement in club manufacture from the days of the hickory-shaft to the modern clubs which are made of a great variety of materials.

The magic which the golfer is looking for from new equipment, sadly, does not always last long. But who cares. Golf is a game of anticipation and tomorrow is when it will all happen. If not tomorrow, the next day will have to do.

Clubs and balls are governed by Rules 4 and 5 and Appendices II and III of the Rules of Golf.

Opposite John Daly unleashes his 'killer whale' driver from the 6th tee at Muirfield during the 1992 Open Championship.

Below Rake irons old (c 1895) and new; non-conforming.

Any furrows in or runners on the sole shall not extend into the face. (Appendix II, 4-1 d)

Above Bobby Jones playing in 1927.

The player shall start a 'stipulated round' with not more than fourteen clubs. (Rule 4-4a)

The question often asked is: Why fourteen clubs? The truth is that nobody really knows, but it reached a point in the 1930s where enough was enough. It is alleged that Tony Torrance had a long conversation with Bobby Jones about the limitation of the number of clubs, in the car park at Pine Valley during the 1936 Walker Cup Match. One of the American team, Scotty Campbell, had thirty-two clubs including seven niblicks. Bobby asked Tony how many clubs he had in his bag and Tony said 'twelve'. Bobby said 'I was carrying sixteen in 1930' so they compromised with fourteen.

The USGA put the fourteen-club limit in the Rules in 1938, but the R&A Membership refused to go along with this suggestion until 1939.

Right The late Harry Busson of Walton Heath – a traditional club-maker.

A manufacturer may submit to the Royal and Ancient Golf Club of St Andrews a sample of a club which is to be manufactured for a ruling as to whether the club conforms with Rule 4 and Appendix II. (Preamble to Rule 4)

Right Duffy Waldorf asks his wife and children to write messages of encouragement on his golf balls.

The responsibility for playing the proper ball rests with the player. Each player should put an identification mark on his ball. (Rule 12-2)

Below Colin Montgomerie inspects his ball for damage.

A ball is unfit for play if it is visibly cut, cracked or out of shape. A ball is not unfit for play solely because mud or other materials adhere to it, its surface is scratched or scraped or its paint is damaged or discoloured. (Rule 5-3)

Starter to player 'Can you identify your ball?'
'Yes', replied the player with certainty. 'I am playing a Titleist No 2'.
'Quite', said the starter. 'But can you identify it?'
'Yes, I've just told you so', repeated the player.
'My good man', said the starter, 'You don't seem to understand. Suppose you drove on to another fairway, or some other player drove on to your fairway, and they were also playing a Titleist No 2, could you tell which ball was yours?'
As though the penny had dropped the player said 'I see what you mean and I tell you what I will do. If there are so many people out there playing a No 2, I will change and play a No 3'.

Right and below Tiger Woods and John Daly, two of the longest hitters of the modern game, can use clubs with shafts made of steel, graphite or titanium, to name but three materials.

Steel shafts were permitted for the first time in 1929, a change which prompted Robert Harris, Chairman of the Golf Ball Sub-Committee of the R&A's Rules Committee in the 1930s, to comment some years later:

'With the legalising of steel shafts there began another flurry and flutter in the game. It was soon realised by players that the rigid steel shaft could not be made to work to the same extent as hickory with its torsion qualities...The soullessness of metal took the finesse out of the game – a new, more stereotyped method of hit had to be found.'

122

Opposite Laura Davies acknowledged as the longest hitter in the women's game.

Right Mark Calcavecchia consults a yardage book and a hole location chart to help his club selection.

A player may ask anyone to inform him as to the distance from a permanent object to another permanent object (eg from a tee board to a fairway bunker, from a tree to a water hazard, from a sprinkler head to a putting green, etc). Such information is public information. (Decision 8-1/2)

Insets Many clubs in one – adjustable iron clubs (c 1900); non-conforming.

The club shall not be designed to be adjustable except for weight. (Rule 4-1a)

During a 'stipulated round', the playing characteristics of a club shall not be purposely changed by adjustment or by any other means. (Rule 4-2)

Above Bernhard Langer loses hold of his wedge as he blasts out of the Wentworth rough during the 1996 Volvo PGA Championship.

Right Ben Crenshaw uses a 3-iron on the green during his singles match against Eamonn Darcy in the 1987 Ryder Cup. Crenshaw's putter broke earlier in the round after he hit the head of the putter on the ground.

A club which is damaged 'other than in the normal course of play' may not be repaired or replaced during the round. (Rules 4-1g, 4-2 and 4-4a)

There is nothing in the Rules to say you must use a putter (*a club designed primarily for use on the putting green*) on the green, or that you cannot use a putter off the green.

During the Open Championship at St Andrews in 1995 three players decided to play a wedge on the green, but forgot to have the flagstick attended. Fortunately no one struck the flagstick, otherwise he would have incurred a two-stroke penalty. (Rule 17-3c)

Right Player keeps those grooves clean.

A series of straight grooves with diverging sides and a symmetrical cross-section may be used. Also, punch marks may be used. (Appendix II, 4-1e)

Below Gary Player earned a reputation for fine bunker play.

In 1922 the Rules of Golf Committee decided on a standard measurement for a ball of 'not less than 1.62 inches in diameter by not more than 1.62 ounces in weight'. The USGA after several meetings with the R&A adopted, in 1929, a specification of 1.68 inches in diameter and 1.55 ounces in weight. However, this standard was soon abandoned as providing too light a ball, after which the Americans' specification became 1.68 inches in diameter and 1.62 ounces in weight. No agreement on a uniform ball could be reached at this time.

As with most matters of disagreement a compromise was suggested and experiments were made with a ball of 1.66 inches in diameter. The debate about the 'ball' was to continue, but a compromise could not be reached. It would not be until the 1st January 1990 that the small 1.62 inches ball would become illegal and the 1.68 inches in diameter ball would be uniform throughout the world.

During the period of the experimental 1.66 inches ball John Salvesen, a Past Captain of the R&A had the unique achievement of having three 'holes in one', on three different Continents with three different sizes of ball.

The first was in Europe, with a 7-iron at the 11th hole on the Old Course, St Andrews, using a 1.66 inches in diameter ball.

The second was in Africa with a driver at the 18th hole using a 1.62 inches in diameter ball, during the 75th celebration of the Royal Salisbury Golf Club, now Royal Harare. He still has the ball together with a photostat copy of the bar statement for the two days they thought he deserved.

The third was in North America at the Westwood Golf Club, on what is known as the Lakeland 9 holes. He holed a 3-wood at the 9th hole (his 18th of the round) using a 1.68 inches in diameter ball.

HOW WOULD YOU RULE?
A Rules official in a buggy accidentally ran over a player's ball. In his excitement he reversed and backed over the player's clubs, breaking two of them in the process. May the player replace the clubs?

127

Left Gene Sarazen, inventor of the sand wedge in 1932, continues to play well out of bunkers.

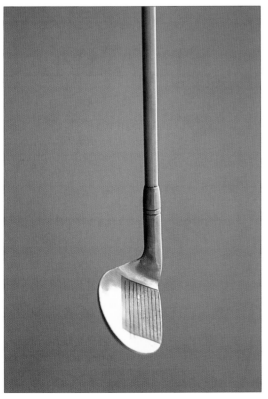

Far left A modern illegal sand iron.

The face of the club shall not have any degree of concavity. (Rule 4-1e)

Left A water niblick from the 1880s; non-conforming.

Holes through the head are not permitted. (Appendix II, 4-1d)

Left and right Sam Torrance uses a long putter (54 inches) while Barry Lane prefers a much shorter club (31 inches).

A club must be at least 18 inches in length. (Appendix II, 4-1b)

Below Bernhard Langer uses a putter designed by Dave Pelz in 1986. It was ruled that this putter contravened Rule 4-1d, ie the distance from heel to toe of the clubhead must measure more than from face to back.

Torrance's 'broomhandle' putter conforms to the Rules. Not all of them do.

About 1970 a golfer returned from a curling holiday in Switzerland having noticed that several curlers used brooms whose handles were hollow and contained whisky. He asked the R&A whether a putter of the same design would be legal. The following is an extract* from the reply composed by Stewart Lawson, a former Chairman of the Committee:-

*The complete poem can be found on page 192.

A drouthy lot, the curling crew!
Their broomstick tops they can unscrew
And fill the shaft with barley-broo;
 Does 'soop' mean 'sweep' or 'sup'?
Now, could a thirsty golfer use,
Without offence, a putter whose
True-temper shaft was filled with booze
 To keep his spirits up?

And so, on balance, we're inclined
To rule against a club designed
For holding drink of any kind;
 A putter most of all.
For just suppose, in rage or grief,
One broke the shaft, it's our belief
Rule 32 gives no relief
 From casual alcohol!

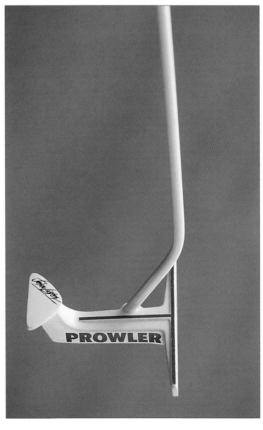

Top left This putter in the shape of a foot and was ruled against on the grounds that it was not *traditional and customary* (Rule 4-1a)

Top right The addition of a golf ball to the toe and heel of this putter meant that it was not *generally plain in shape* (Rule 4-1d).

Bottom right The 'Prowler' with its aircraft like tail fin, is not considered to be *plain in shape*. (Appendix II, 4-1d)

Bottom left The Schenectady putter (c1903) was one of the earliest clubs to fall foul of the Rules. The centre-shafted putter was used by American Walter Travis to win the Amateur Championship at Sandwich in 1904. However, in 1909 the R&A banned the use of a croquet mallet as a putter and one year later this ban was extended to all 'mallet-like clubs' ie only clubs that had the shaft attached to the heel of the clubhead were allowed. The R&A's ban on centre-shafted putters lasted 42 years until the first joint code of Rules with the USGA in 1952.

WIDE WORLD OF GOLF

PLAY THE COURSE AS YOU FIND IT AND THE BALL AS IT LIES.
IF YOU CANNOT DO EITHER, DO WHAT IS FAIR.
BUT TO DO WHAT IS FAIR YOU HAVE TO KNOW THE RULES.

H OW MANY GAMES are there where the ordinary players can compare their own standard with that of the 'stars'? The great players play the same courses with the same equipment and with the benefit of a handicap one might even give them a good game. And what's more, both could enjoy it. The 1st hole on the Old Course at St Andrews is the same whether you are playing in the Open or are playing with your friends while on holiday. The only thing which is different is the occasion.

There are few countries in the world where golf is not played and it is currently one of the fastest growing sports. The fact that the game can never be mastered may be one of the reasons the golfer keeps coming back for more and more and more. The game is played in some of the loveliest parts of the world and there is an immense amount of pleasure to be had and a great deal of fun.

Golf must be one of the few games where those who play it are prepared to carry their sporting equipment, sometimes vast distances. They are willing to part with substantial sums of money just to be able to play and are not too upset if they play badly or the weather is less than perfect.

Furthermore, it is a game where the players are responsible for knowing and applying the Rules. Golfers are expected to apply the Rules without fault or favour and call a penalty on themselves if they have committed an error.

As early as 1908 the R&A felt that the Rules of Golf should be available free of charge, a decision that led to the remarkable sponsorship by Royal Insurance (now Royal Sun Alliance) which continues to this day, the company being responsible for the printing and distribution of all copies in the English language.

Almost four million copies of the Rules are circulated in English and they are also published in twenty-four other languages - it is truly a wide world of golf.

It may be fair to say that you either love the game of golf or you hate it. It is even possible both to love it and hate it.

Opposite An autumnal view of the 1st hole of the Great White Course at the Greenbrier Club in West Virginia.

The Committee may make a temporary Local Rule declaring accumulations of leaves through the green at certain holes to be ground under repair and Rule 25-1 will apply. (Decision 33-8/31)

NORTH AMERICA

Opposite The par-4 18th hole at Pine Valley.

Left Desert golf in Arizona involves playing over and around large boulders.

Stones of any size (which are not solidly embedded) are loose impediments and may be removed, provided play is not unduly delayed. (Decision 23-1/2)

Spectators, caddies, fellow-competitors, etc may assist a player in removing a large loose impediment. (Decision 23-1/3)

Below Teeing off into the morning desert sun at Troon North Golf Club, Phoenix, Arizona.

The par-4 8th hole on the Palmer Course at Mission Hills Country Club, Palm Springs, California.

If an overhead power line is so situated that a perfectly played shot can be deflected, the Committee may make a Local Rule requiring the player to cancel and replay the stroke. (Decision 33-8/13)

Above Alligators beside the 2nd green at Lake Nona, Florida.

Golf is not meant to be a dangerous game. It has been said that if you are confronted with a crocodile or an alligator you should remember that they can both run very fast but do not turn quickly.

Two elderly men were playing one day when suddenly an alligator appeared in front of them.

'What are we supposed to do?' enquired one from the other.

'We run 10 yards forward, turn at right angles and then run like hell,' replied his friend.

'But I do not run fast,' said the first man.

'You don't have to run fast' said the friend. 'All you have to do is beat me.'

Right Both fishermen and golfers are prone to exaggeration and talk of the 'ones that got away'.

Far right Perhaps the largest staked tree in the world?

Left The Banff Springs Golf Club in the Rocky Mountains, Canada.

Below A 'skins game' in the desert creates a traffic jam.

A Rules official called for a second opinion having denied a player relief from casual water. The 'rover' duly arrived in his buggy, coming to a grinding halt, and asked:
'What's the problem and where's the ball?'
The Rules official replied, 'The problem is now a little more serious because the ball is under your front wheel.'

EUROPE

Opposite Hazards galore at Cruden Bay in Scotland. A burn, numerous bunkers, humps and hollows, deep rough and the North Sea combine to test the golfer.

Left Rye Golf Club in winter. Home of the President's Putter, an annual match play competition for members of the Oxford and Cambridge Golf Society which is played in the first week of January when the weather in England is not at its best. In 1983 there was an unusual Rules incident when a player's ball at rest on the putting green was struck by a flagstick. The flagstick had been removed from the hole and placed on the green. The player was about to putt when a sudden and fierce gust of wind lifted the flagstick as if it was a piece of straw and blew it across the green against the player's ball.

Rule 17-3 imposes a penalty for a ball striking a flagstick which has been removed from the hole, but makes no provision for the converse. It was ruled that the flagstick was an 'outside agency' and the ball was replaced without penalty. (Decision 18-1/6)

Below The 10th hole at Valderrama, Spain, venue of the 1997 Ryder Cup.

Right The par-3 11th hole at Royal Ashdown Forest Golf Club in Sussex, England.

Below Late afternoon shadows cross the 11th fairway on the West Course at the Wentworth Club in Surrey, England.

Around 1888 it was decided 'that in order to meet the wishes of the English Golf Clubs, who desire to obtain uniformity of the Rules for Golf by the verbatim adoption of the Rules approved by the Royal and Ancient Golf Club, the Royal and Ancient Golf Club extract from the main body of their Rules those relating to such local accidents as the Swilcan Burn, the Eden and the Station Master's Garden, and so group these under a separate heading, so that the main body of the Rules may be used wherever the game of golf is or shall be played.'

Above The 3rd and 4th holes of the Championship Course at Royal County Down in Northern Ireland stretch out toward the Mountains of Mourne.

Left The 15th hole at Portmarnock, near Dublin.

On his first visit to Portmarnock in 1960, John Scrivener, who later became Chairman of the Rules Committee (1990-1995), walked onto the 15th tee. He placed the cigarette he was smoking on the ground and prepared to play his tee-shot. However, before he could do so, a strong gust of wind blew the cigarette towards the beach and out of bounds, whereupon he announced 'I'd better light a provisional!'

The par-4 8th (in the foreground) and 11th holes at the European Club, Brittas Bay, Wicklow, Ireland.

Right Aroeira Golf Club near Lisbon, Portugal.

Opposite The 18th hole at the Golf Club de Bossy in France.

Below Michael Jonzon at Crans-sur-Sierre, Switzerland.

Left Bernhard Langer surveys his next shot during the 1996 German Open in Munich.

Bernard Langer writes:
'The game of golf has always been known as a game played by gentlemen, in a fair way. What other sport is there, where you play for hundreds of thousands of dollars and the players penalize themselves? The rules we have were revised many times, but the true spirit of a fair game has always been the focal point.'

Opposite John Daly at the 1996 Scandinavian Masters in Sweden.

Below Bernhard Langer employs his coach as his caddie for the 1996 German Open.

There is no restriction in the Rules of Golf as to whom a player may employ as his caddie. Restrictions may be imposed by a Committee, however, in the conditions of a competition. (Decision 6-4/2)

The 2nd green at Royal Mougins Golf Club in Cannes, Southern France.

ASIA

Above Horses crossing a fairway at Hong Kong Golf Club.

Above inset 'Out of bounds to horses'!

On courses used by horses the following Local Rules may be introduced:

Although 'dung' is, by definition, a loose impediment it may be declared, by the Committee, to be ground under repair (Rule 25-1 applies).

'Hoof marks' may be declared to be ground under repair, however, by Local Rule the Committee is authorised to deny a player relief from interference with his stance (Note to Rule 25-1).

Left An old bus serves as the Recorders Office at Hong Kong Golf Club.

The competitor is responsible for the correctness of the score recorded for each hole on his card. (Rule 6-6d)

Right The practice putting green at Gotemba Golf Club in Japan.

On any day of a stroke play competition, a competitor must not practise on the competition course or test the surface of any putting green on the course before a round. (Rule 7-1b) However, practice putting or chipping on or near the 1st tee is permitted. (Exception 1 to Rule 7-1b)

Below The 3-tiered Shiba driving range in Tokyo, full of eager golfers even after dark.

Above Jose Maria Olazabal at Fujiyama Golf Club, Japan.

Below A caddie in Japan often looks after more than one player.

When one caddie is employed by more than one player, he is always deemed to be the caddie of the player whose ball is involved, and equipment carried by him is deemed to be that player's equipment, except when the caddie acts upon specific directions of another player, in which case he is considered to be that other player's caddie. (Definition)

Above Brooms are used to help maintain the bunkers at the 1992 Dunlop Phoenix Tournament in Miyazaki, Japan.

Left Golfers repair their divot holes, or if you're lucky someone will do it for you.

Opposite Jumbo Ozaki, Japan's top golfer attracts a large crowd whenever he plays in Japan.

The 18th green at the Blue Canyon Country Club in Thailand.

Above Ernie Els receives a colourful welcome on his arrival in Manila for the 1995 Johnnie Walker Classic.

Left Local caddies at the Seoul Country Club, South Korea.

Opposite Jack Kay plays from a bunker in Bali, Indonesia during the 1994 Alfred Dunhill Masters.

Jack Kay's victory in Bali was somewhat overshadowed by the disqualification of Nick Faldo on the 12th green of the final round. Faldo was six shots clear of the field when it was discovered that he had unwittingly breached Rule 13-4 during the 3rd round by removing a piece of coral from a bunker.

The penalty for a breach of Rule 13-4 is, in stroke play, two strokes, but because Faldo's error was not discovered until the following day, he was disqualified for returning a score lower than actually taken (Rule 6-6d).

An island green at Mission Hills Golf Club, Thailand.

If a putting green is situated on an island in a lake, the Committee might consider establishing a dropping zone and adopting a Local Rule giving a player, whose ball lies in the hazard, the option of dropping a ball in the dropping zone, under penalty of one stroke. (Decision 33-2a/10)

AUSTRALIA

Above Joondalup Golf Club in Perth, Western Australia, with its resident kangaroos.

Right The 5th hole of the 'composite course' at Royal Melbourne, where players are encouraged to wheel their trolleys across rather than around the greens.

Left The 5th hole at the New South Wales Club is bordered by the waters of Botany Bay.

Ian Baker-Finch has this to say about the happy helper who phones in to officials and who causes the disqualification of a player who inadvertently and unintentionally breaks a Rule. 'If a Rule is broken on course and the player is unaware of such a breach and signs his card, hands it in, and later finds out about the breach of Rule, he should be given a 2-stroke penalty, or as the particular Rule states, and not be disqualified.

'The DQ Rule in many cases causes delay because the players are unable to implement their own interpretation of a ruling for fear of disqualification. What happened in the days before on-course officials? Until recently in Australian tournaments a player would play two balls if he was unsure of a Rule, and ask for a ruling after play was completed. I think this is a far better way of handling this situation and also keeps play moving as we are all aware with the difficulty of today's modern courses, slow play is a major concern.'

Below The 16th hole at Kingston Heath Golf Club, another of Melbourne's famous sand belt courses.

The long 5th hole at Meadow Springs Golf Club, just south of Perth, Western Australia.

SOUTHERN AFRICA

The 'crocodile pit' on the short 12th hole at the Lost City Course in Sun City, South Africa.

As players are not encouraged to enter the pond for obvious reasons and given that the ground behind the hazard is very rough, a dropping zone is established for those players who fail to carry the pond.

DANGER
DO NOT APPROACH OR ENTER THE
CROCODILE POND
SUN CITY NOT LIABLE FOR ANY LOSS
DAMAGE OR OTHER MISFORTUNE

Above Caddies in the Ivory Coast hold a putting competition while waiting for a bag.

Right A young greenkeeper supplements his wages selling balls found in the long grass in the Ivory Coast.

Below Good advice!

HOW WOULD YOU RULE?

A player in a match found his ball on the edge of the fairway. He took his stance in the rough and was at the top of his backswing when he noticed a snake glide out of the long grass. It passed between his legs and reared its head slightly, eyeing the ball with interest, as if trying to decide whether the ball might be an egg.

Not surprisingly, the player changed his point of aim from the ball to the snake's head. Impact and follow-through were executed and the snake was killed. All seemed well until his opponent said 'good shot'.

The par-5 10th (right) and par-3 17th holes at the Fancourt Country Club, South Africa.

REST OF THE WORLD

Right and Below Desert golf as it used to be throughout the Middle East. At the Dubai Country Club there is no grass from tee to green and the greens are 'browns'.

Putting browns are sand greens and they require special Local Rules. In 1986 there were approximately 500 Clubs playing on this type of putting surface in Australia. Accordingly, the Australian Golf Union issued a standard set of Local Rules which included permission, when the ball lies on or within one club-length of the putting green, to smooth the line from the player's ball to the hole. In fact the green must be smoothed at least one club-length beyond the hole. The 'smoother' must be used lightly and the player must not 'ridge or heap' the sand to his possible advantage.

Also a special Local Rule for lifting, marking and replacing the ball was introduced because a conventional ball-marker would be moved during the smoothing process. This involves the scratching of two straight lines in the sand from the ball and after the smoothing, the original position of the ball is established by projecting these lines back to the point of intersection.

168

Right The 10th hole at the Emirates Golf Club in Dubai, the first grass Course in the Middle East.

On courses such as the Emirates Golf Club it is important to know which areas of sand are bunkers (ie a 'hazard') and which are not (ie 'through the green').

Below Floodlit golf at Dubai Horse Racing and Golf Club where golf can be played on the Course inside the race track from 7 am until midnight every day of the year.

A relatively recent phenomenon, floodlit golf has proved popular in those parts of the world where it is not possible to play golf in the evening without artificial lighting.

A floodlight pole is an immovable obstruction from which relief, without penalty, is available (Rule 24-2 and Decision 24-2b/3)

If a ball in motion is deflected by a floodlight pole, it is a 'rub of the green' and the ball must be played as it lies, without penalty. (Rule 19-1)

169

The Dubai Creek Course and Clubhouse. The Clubhouse was designed in the style of an Arabian dhow.

Right Course maintenance can be a labour intensive job. A 'push pull' mower is used to cut the tees in India.

When a ball lies near a washing tub, or implements used in the up-keep of the Links, they may be removed and when on clothes, the ball may be lifted and dropped behind them, without penalty. (c 1888)

Below 'Synchronised mowing' at Augusta as part of the meticulous preparations for the Masters Tournament.

172

A 'closely mown area' means any area of the course, including paths through the rough, cut to fairway height or less. (Rule 25-2)

Above Cabo de Sol Golf Club in Mexico.

Left Practising in Lima, Peru, under the watchful eye of the local police.

In an attempt to discourage trespassers looking for balls, a club passed a bye-law that after 5 minutes search any lost ball belonged to the club. A lawyer did his best to dissuade the club from doing this because it was not based on natural justice. He pointed out that if such a bye-law applied to a golf ball it must also apply to anything else. For example, suppose you lost your mother-in-law for more than 5 minutes it might even surprise her to be told that she had become club property. Such an option would be too attractive to many members and visitors would willingly pay a substantial green fee for the chance.

The Gavea Club in Rio de Janeiro, Brazil.

The 'Suggestion Box' at the St Andrews Course, Hamilton Golf Club, New Zealand.

The Rules of Golf

28TH EDITION EFFECTIVE 1ST JANUARY 1996

Section I: ETIQUETTE

COURTESY ON THE COURSE

Safety

Prior to playing a stroke or making a practice swing, the player should ensure that no one is standing close by or in a position to be hit by the club, the ball or any stones, pebbles, twigs or the like which may be moved by the stroke or swing.

Consideration for Other Players

The player who has the honour should be allowed to play before his opponent or fellow-competitor tees his ball.

No one should move, talk or stand close to or directly behind the ball or the hole when a player is addressing the ball or making a stroke.

No player should play until the players in front are out of range.

Pace of Play

In the interest of all, players should play without delay.

Players searching for a ball should signal the players behind them to pass as soon as it becomes apparent that the ball will not easily be found. They should not search for five minutes before doing so. They should not continue play until the players following them have passed and are out of range.

When the play of a hole has been completed, players should immediately leave the putting green.

If a match fails to keep its place on the course and loses more than one clear hole on the players in front, it should invite the match following to pass.

Priority on the Course

In the absence of special rules, two-ball matches should have precedence over and be entitled to pass any three- or four-ball match, which should invite them through.

A single player has no standing and should give way to a match of any kind.

Any match playing a whole round is entitled to pass a match playing a shorter round.

CARE OF THE COURSE

Holes in Bunkers

Before leaving a bunker, a player should carefully fill up and smooth over all holes and footprints made by him.

Replace Divots; Repair Ball-Marks and Damage by Spikes

Through the green, a player should ensure that any turf cut or displaced by him is replaced at once and pressed down and that any damage to the putting green made by a ball is carefully repaired. *On completion of the hole* by all players in the group, damage to the putting green caused by golf shoe spikes should be repaired.

Damage to Greens – Flagsticks, Bags, etc.

Players should ensure that, when putting down bags or the flagstick, no damage is done to the putting green and that neither they nor their caddies damage the hole by standing close to it, in handling the flagstick or in removing the ball from the hole. The flagstick should be properly replaced in the hole before the players leave the putting green. Players should not damage the putting green by leaning on their putters, particularly when removing the ball from the hole.

Golf Carts

Local notices regulating the movement of golf carts should be strictly observed.

Damage Through Practice Swings

In taking practice swings, players should avoid causing damage to the course, particularly the tees, by removing divots.

Section II: DEFINITIONS

The Definitions are placed in alphabetical order and some are also repeated at the beginning of their relevant Rule.

In the Rules themselves, defined terms which may be important to the application of a Rule are underlined the first time they appear.

Addressing the Ball

A player has "addressed the ball" when he has taken his stance and has also grounded his club, except that in a hazard a player has addressed the ball when he has taken his stance.

Advice

"Advice" is any counsel or suggestion which could influence a player in determining his play, the choice of a club or the method of making a stroke.

Information on the Rules or on matters of public information, such as the position of hazards or the flagstick on the putting green, is not advice.

Ball Deemed to Move

See "Move or Moved".

Ball Holed

See "Holed".

Ball Lost

See "Lost Ball".

Ball in Play

A ball is "in play" as soon as the player has made a stroke on the teeing ground. It remains in play until holed out, except when it is lost, out of bounds or lifted, or another ball has been substituted whether or not such substitution is permitted; a ball so substituted becomes the ball in play.

Bunker

A "bunker" is a hazard consisting of a prepared area of ground, often a hollow, from which turf or soil has been removed and replaced with sand or the like. Grass-covered ground bordering or within a bunker is not part of the bunker. The margin of a bunker extends vertically downwards, but not upwards. A ball is in a bunker when it lies in or any part of it touches the bunker.

Caddie

A "caddie" is one who carries or handles a player's clubs during play and otherwise assists him in accordance with the Rules.

When one caddie is employed by more than one player, he is always deemed to be the caddie of the player whose ball is involved, and equipment carried by him is deemed to be that player's equipment, except when the caddie acts upon specific directions of another player, in which case he is considered to be that other player's caddie.

Casual Water

"Casual water" is any temporary accumulation of water on the course which is visible before or after the player takes his stance and is not in a water hazard. Snow and natural ice, other than frost, are either casual water or loose impediments, at the option of the player. Manufactured ice is an obstruction. Dew and frost are not casual water. A ball is in casual water when it lies in or any part of it touches the casual water.

Committee

The "Committee" is the committee in charge of the competition or, if the matter does not arise in a competition, the committee in charge of the course.

Competitor

A "competitor" is a player in a stroke competition. A "fellow-competitor" is any person with whom the competitor plays. Neither is partner of the other.

In stroke play foursome and four-ball competitions, where the context so admits, the word "competitor" or "fellow-competitor" includes his partner.

Course

The "course" is the whole area within which play is permitted (see Rule 33-2).

Equipment

"Equipment" is anything used, worn or carried by or for the player except any ball he has played at the hole being played and any small object, such as a coin or a tee, when used to mark the position of a ball or the extent of an area in which a ball is to be dropped. Equipment includes a golf cart, whether or not motorised. If such a cart is shared by two or more players, the cart and everything in it are deemed to be the equipment of the player whose ball is involved except that, when the cart is being moved by one of the players sharing it, the cart and everything in it are deemed to be that player's equipment.

Note: A ball played at the hole being played is equipment when it has been lifted and not put back into play.

Fellow-Competitor

See "Competitor".

Flagstick

The "flagstick" is a movable straight indicator, with or without bunting or other material attached, centred in the hole to show its position. It shall be circular in cross-section.

Forecaddie

A "forecaddie" is one who is employed by the Committee to indicate to players the position of balls during play. He is an outside agency.

Ground Under Repair

"Ground under repair" is any portion of the course so marked by order of the Committee or so declared by its authorised representative. It includes material piled for removal and a hole made by a greenkeeper, even if not so marked. Stakes and lines defining ground under repair are in such ground. Stakes defining ground under repair are obstructions. The margin of ground under repair extends vertically downwards, but not upwards. A ball is in ground under repair when it lies in or any part of it touches the ground under repair.

Note 1: Grass cuttings and other material left on the course which have been abandoned and are not intended to be removed are not ground under repair unless so marked.

Note 2: The Committee may make a Local Rule prohibiting play from ground under repair or an environmentally-sensitive area which has been defined as ground under repair.

Hazards

A "hazard" is any bunker or water hazard.

Hole

The "hole" shall be 4¼ inches (108mm) in diameter and at least 4 inches (100mm) deep. If a lining is used, it shall be sunk at least 1 inch (25mm) below the putting green surface unless the nature of the soil makes it impracticable to do so; its outer diameter shall not exceed 4¼ inches (108mm).

Holed

A ball is "holed" when it is at rest within the circumference of the hole and all of it is below the level of the lip of the hole.

Honour

The side entitled to play first from the teeing ground is said to have the "honour".

Lateral Water Hazard

A "lateral water hazard" is a water hazard or that part of a water hazard so situated that it is not possible or is deemed by the Committee to be impracticable to drop a ball behind the water hazard in accordance with Rule 26-1b.

That part of a water hazard to be played as a lateral water hazard should be distinctively marked. A ball is in a lateral water hazard when it lies in or any part of it touches the lateral water hazard.

Note 1: Lateral water hazards should be defined by red stakes or lines.

Note 2: The Committee may make a Local Rule prohibiting play from an environmentally-sensitive area which has been defined as a lateral water hazard.

Line of Play

The "line of play" is the direction which the player wishes his ball to take after a stroke,

plus a reasonable distance on either side of the intended direction. The line of play extends vertically upwards from the ground, but does not extend beyond the hole.

Line of Putt

The "line of putt" is the line which the player wishes his ball to take after a stroke on the putting green. Except with respect to Rule 16-1e, the line of putt includes a reasonable distance on either side of the intended line. The line of putt does not extend beyond the hole.

Loose Impediments

"Loose impediments" are natural objects such as stones, leaves, twigs, branches and the like, dung, worms and insects and casts or heaps made by them, provided they are not fixed or growing, are not solidly embedded and do not adhere to the ball.

Sand and loose soil are loose impediments on the putting green, but not elsewhere.

Snow and natural ice, other than frost, are either casual water or loose impediments, at the option of the player. Manufactured ice is an obstruction.

Dew and frost are not loose impediments.

Lost Ball

A ball is "lost" if:

a. It is not found or identified as his by the player within five minutes after the player's side or his or their caddies have begun to search for it; or

b. The player has put another ball into play under the Rules, even though he may not have searched for the original ball; or

c. The player has played any stroke with a provisional ball from the place where the original ball is likely to be or from a point nearer the hole than that place, whereupon the provisional ball becomes the ball in play.

Time spent in playing a wrong ball is not counted in the five-minute period allowed for search.

Marker

A "marker" is one who is appointed by the Committee to record a competitor's score in stroke play. He may be a fellow-competitor. He is not a referee.

Matches

See "Sides and Matches".

Move or Moved

A ball is deemed to have "moved" if it leaves its position and comes to rest in any other place.

Observer

An "observer" is one who is appointed by the Committee to assist a referee to decide questions of fact and to report to him any breach of a Rule. An observer should not attend the flagstick, stand at or mark the position of the hole, or lift the ball or mark its position.

Obstructions

An "obstruction" is anything artificial, including the artificial surfaces and sides of roads and paths and manufactured ice, except:

a. Objects defining out of bounds, such as walls, fences, stakes and railings;

b. Any part of an immovable artificial object which is out of bounds; and

c. Any construction declared by the Committee to be an integral part of the course.

Out of Bounds

"Out of bounds" is ground on which play is prohibited.

When out of bounds is defined by reference to stakes or a fence or as being beyond stakes or a fence, the out of bounds line is determined by the nearest inside points of the stakes or fence posts at ground level excluding angled supports.

When out of bounds is defined by a line on the ground, the line itself is out of bounds.

The out of bounds line extends vertically upwards and downwards.

A ball is out of bounds when all of it lies out of bounds.

A player may stand out of bounds to play a ball lying within bounds.

Outside Agency

An "outside agency" is any agency not part of the match or, in stroke play, not part of the competitor's side, and includes a referee, a marker, an observer and a forecaddie. Neither wind nor water is an outside agency.

Partner

A "partner" is a player associated with another player on the same side.

In a threesome, foursome, best-ball or four-ball match, where the context so admits, the word "player" includes his partner or partners.

Penalty Stroke

A "penalty stroke" is one added to the score of a player or side under certain Rules. In a threesome or foursome, penalty strokes do not affect the order of play.

Provisional Ball

A "provisional ball" is a ball played under Rule 27-2 for a ball which may be lost outside a water hazard or may be out of bounds.

Putting Green

The "putting green" is all ground of the hole being played which is specially prepared for putting or otherwise defined as such by the Committee. A ball is on the putting green when any part of it touches the putting green.

Referee

A "referee" is one who is appointed by the Committee to accompany players to decide questions of fact and apply the Rules. He shall act on any breach of a Rule which he observes or is reported to him.

A referee should not attend the flagstick, stand at or mark the position of the hole, or lift the ball or mark its position.

Rub of the Green

A "rub of the green" occurs when a ball in motion is accidentally deflected or stopped by any outside agency (see Rule 19-1).

Rule

The term "Rule" includes Local Rules made by the Committee under Rule 33-8a.

Sides and Matches

Side: A player, or two or more players who are partners.

Single: A match in which one plays against another.

Threesome: A match in which one plays against two, and each side plays one ball.

Foursome: A match in which two play against two, and each side plays one ball.

Three-ball: A match play competition in which three play against one another, each playing his own ball. Each player is playing two distinct matches.

Best-ball: A match in which one plays against the better ball of two or the best ball of three players.

Four-ball: A match in which two play their better ball against the better ball of two other players.

Stance

Taking the "stance" consists in a player placing his feet in position for and preparatory to making a stroke.

Stipulated Round

The "stipulated round" consists of playing the holes of the course in their correct sequence unless otherwise authorised by the Committee. The number of holes in a stipulated round is 18 unless a smaller number is authorised by the Committee. As to extension of stipulated round in match play, see Rule 2-3.

Stroke

A "stroke" is the forward movement of the club made with the intention of fairly striking at and moving the ball, but if a player checks his downswing voluntarily before the clubhead reaches the ball he is deemed not to have made a stroke.

Teeing Ground

The "teeing ground" is the starting place for the hole to be played. It is a rectangular area two club-lengths in depth, the front and the sides of which are defined by the outside limits of two tee-markers. A ball is outside the teeing ground when all of it lies outside the teeing ground.

Through the Green

"Through the green" is the whole area of the course except:

a. The teeing ground and putting green of the hole being played; and

b. All hazards on the course.

Water Hazard

A "water hazard" is any sea, lake, pond, river, ditch, surface drainage ditch or other open water course (whether or not containing water) and anything of a similar nature.

All ground or water within the margin of a water hazard is part of the water hazard. The margin of a water hazard extends vertically upwards and downwards. Stakes and lines defining the margins of water hazards are in the hazards. Such stakes are obstructions. A ball is in a water hazard when it lies in or any part of it touches the water hazard.

Note 1: Water hazards (other than lateral water hazards) should be defined by yellow stakes or lines.

Note 2: The Committee may make a Local Rule prohibiting play from an environmentally-sensitive area which has been defined as a water hazard.

Wrong Ball

A "wrong ball" is any ball other than the player's:

a. Ball in play,

b. Provisional ball, or

c. Second ball played under Rule 3-3 or Rule 20-7b in stroke play.

Note: Ball in play includes a ball substituted for the ball in play whether or not such substitution is permitted.

Section III: THE GAME

RULE 1. THE GAME

1-1.   General

The Game of Golf consists in playing a ball from the teeing ground into the hole by a stroke or successive strokes in accordance with the Rules.

1-2.   Exerting Influence on Ball

No player or caddie shall take any action to influence the position or the movement of a ball except in accordance with the Rules.

PENALTY FOR BREACH OF RULE 1-2:

Match Play – Loss of hole; Stroke play – Two strokes.

Note: In the case of a serious breach of Rule 1-2, the Committee may impose a penalty of disqualification.

1-3.   Agreement to Waive Rules

Players shall not agree to exclude the operation of any Rule or to waive any penalty incurred.

PENALTY FOR BREACH OF RULE 1-3:

Match play – Disqualification of both sides;
Stroke play – Disqualification of competitors concerned.

(Agreeing to play out of turn in stroke play – see Rule 10-2c.)

1-4.   Points Not Covered by Rules

If any point in dispute is not covered by the Rules, the decision shall be made in accordance with equity.

RULE 2.   MATCH PLAY

2-1.   Winner of Hole; Reckoning of Holes

In match play the game is played by holes.

Except as otherwise provided in the Rules, a hole is won by the side which holes its ball in the fewer strokes. In a handicap match the lower net score wins the hole.

The reckoning of holes is kept by the terms: so many "holes up" or "all square", and so many "to play".

A side is "dormie" when it is as many holes up as there are holes remaining to be played.

2-2.   Halved Hole

A hole is halved if each side holes out in the same number of strokes.

When a player has holed out and his opponent has been left with a stroke for the half, if the player thereafter incurs a penalty, the hole is halved.

2-3.   Winner of Match

A match (which consists of a stipulated round, unless otherwise decreed by the Committee) is won by the side which is leading by a number of holes greater than the number of holes remaining to be played.

The Committee may, for the purpose of settling a tie, extend the stipulated round to as many holes as are required for a match to be won.

2-4.   Concession of Next Stroke, Hole or Match

When the opponent's ball is at rest or is deemed to be at rest under Rule 16-2, the player may concede the opponent to have holed out with his next stroke and the ball may be removed by either side with a club or otherwise.

A player may concede a hole or a match at any time prior to the conclusion of the hole or the match.

Concession of a stroke, hole or match may not be declined or withdrawn.

2-5.   Claims

In match play, if a doubt or dispute arises between the players and no duly authorised representative of the Committee is available within a reasonable time, the players shall continue the match without delay. Any claim, if it is to be considered by the Committee, must be made before any player in the match plays from the next teeing ground or, in the case of the last hole of the match, before all players in the match leave the putting green.

No later claim shall be considered unless it is based on facts previously unknown to the player making the claim and the player making the claim had been given wrong information (Rules 6-2a and

9) by an opponent. In any case, no later claim shall be considered after the result of the match has been officially announced, unless the Committee is satisfied that the opponent knew he was giving wrong information.

2-6. General Penalty
The penalty for a breach of a Rule in match play is loss of hole except when otherwise provided.

RULE 3. STROKE PLAY
3-1. Winner
The competitor who plays the stipulated round or rounds in the fewest strokes is the winner.

3-2. Failure to Hole Out
If a competitor fails to hole out at any hole and does not correct his mistake before he plays a stroke from the next teeing ground or, in the case of the last hole of the round, before he leaves the putting green, *he shall be disqualified.*

3-3. Doubt as to Procedure
a. Procedure
In stroke play only, when during play of a hole a competitor is doubtful of his rights or procedure, he may, without penalty, play a second ball. After the situation which caused the doubt has arisen, the competitor should, before taking further action, announce to his marker or a fellow-competitor his decision to invoke this Rule and the ball with which he will score if the Rules permit.

The competitor shall report the facts to the Committee before returning his score card unless he scores the same with both balls; if he fails to do so, *he shall be disqualified.*

b. Determination of Score for Hole
If the Rules allow the procedure selected in advance by the competitor, the score with the ball selected shall be his score for the hole.

If the competitor fails to announce in advance his decision to invoke this Rule or his selection, the score with the original ball or, if the original ball is not one of the balls being played, the first ball put into play shall count if the Rules allow the procedure adopted for such ball.
Note: A second ball played under Rule 3-3 is not a provisional ball under Rule 27-2.

3-4. Refusal to Comply with a Rule
If a competitor refuses to comply with a Rule affecting the rights of another competitor, *he shall be disqualified.*

3-5. General Penalty
The penalty for a breach of a Rule in stroke play is two strokes except when otherwise provided.

CLUBS AND THE BALL
The Royal and Ancient Golf Club of St. Andrews and the United States Golf Association reserve the right to change the Rules and make and change the interpretations relating to clubs, balls and other implements at any time.

RULE 4. CLUBS
A player in doubt as to the conformity of a club should consult the Royal and Ancient Golf Club of St. Andrews.

A manufacturer may submit to the Royal and Ancient Golf Club of St. Andrews a sample of a club which is to be manufactured for a ruling as to whether the club conforms with Rule 4 and Appendix II. Such sample will become the property of the Royal and Ancient Golf Club of St. Andrews for reference purposes. If a manufacturer fails to submit a sample before manufacturing and/or marketing the club, he assumes the risk of a ruling that the club does not conform with the Rules of Golf.

Where a club, or part of a club, is required to have some specific property, this means that it must be designed and manufactured with the intention of having that property. The finished club or part must have that property within manufacturing tolerances appropriate to the material used.

4-1. Form and Make of Clubs
A club is an implement designed to be used for striking the ball.

A putter is a club with a loft not exceeding ten degrees designed primarily for use on the putting green.

The player's clubs shall conform with the provisions of this Rule and with the specifications and interpretations set forth in Appendix II.
a. General
The club shall be composed of a shaft and a head. All parts of the club shall be fixed so that the club is one unit. The club shall not be designed to be adjustable except for weight (see also Appendix II). The club shall not be substantially different from the traditional and customary form and make, and shall have no external attachments except as otherwise permitted by the Rules.
b. Shaft
The shaft shall be straight, with the same bending and twisting properties in any direction, and shall be attached to the clubhead at the heel either directly or through a single plain neck and/or socket. A putter shaft may be attached to any point in the head.
c. Grip
The grip consists of that part of the shaft designed to be held by the player and any material added to it for the purpose of obtaining a firm hold. The grip shall be straight and plain in form, shall extend to the end of the shaft and shall not be moulded for any part of the hands.
d. Clubhead
The distance from the heel to the toe of the clubhead shall be greater than the distance from the face to the back. The clubhead shall be generally plain in shape.

The clubhead shall have only one striking face, except that a putter may have two such faces if their characteristics are the same, and they are opposite each other.
e. Club Face
The face of the club shall be hard and rigid (some exceptions may be made for putters) and, except for such markings as are permitted by Appendix II, shall be smooth and shall not have any degree of concavity.
f. Wear and Alteration
A club which conforms with Rule 4-1 when new is deemed to conform after wear through normal use. Any part of a club which has been purposely altered is regarded as new and must conform, in the altered state, with the Rules.
g. Damage
If a player's club ceases to conform with Rule 4-1 because of damage sustained in the normal course of play, the player may:
(i) use the club in its damaged state, but only for the remainder of the stipulated round during which such damage was sustained; or

(ii) without unduly delaying play, repair it. A club which ceases to conform because of damage sustained other than in the normal course of play shall not subsequently be used during the round.
(Damage changing playing characteristics of club – see Rule 4-2.)
(Damage rendering club unfit for play – see Rule 4-4a.)

4-2. Playing Characteristics Changed
During a stipulated round, the playing characteristics of a club shall not be purposely changed by adjustment or by any other means.

If the playing characteristics of a player's club are changed during a round because of damage sustained in the normal course of play, the player may:
(i) use the club in its altered state; or
(ii) without unduly delaying play, repair it.

If the playing characteristics of a player's club are changed because of damage sustained other than in the normal course of play, the club shall not subsequently be used during the round.

Damage to a club which occurred prior to a round may be repaired during the round, provided the playing characteristics are not changed and play is not unduly delayed.

4-3. Foreign Material
Foreign material must not be applied to the club face for the purpose of influencing the movement of the ball.
PENALTY FOR BREACH OF RULE 4-1, -2 or -3: *Disqualification.*

4-4. Maximum of Fourteen Clubs
a. Selection and Replacement of Clubs
The player shall start a stipulated round with not more than fourteen clubs. He is limited to the clubs thus selected for that round except that, without unduly delaying play, he may:
(i) if he started with fewer than fourteen clubs, add any number provided his total number does not exceed fourteen; and
(ii) replace, with any club, a club which becomes unfit for play in the normal course of play.

The addition or replacement of a club or clubs may not be made by borrowing any club selected for play by any other person playing on the course.
b. Partners May Share Clubs
Partners may share clubs, provided that the total number of clubs carried by the partners so sharing does not exceed fourteen.
PENALTY FOR BREACH OF RULE 4-4a or b, REGARDLESS OF NUMBER OF EXCESS CLUBS CARRIED:
Match play – At the conclusion of the hole at which the breach is discovered, the state of the match shall be adjusted by deducting one hole for each hole at which a breach occurred. Maximum deduction per round: two holes.
Stroke play – Two strokes for each hole at which any breach occurred; maximum penalty per round: four strokes.
Bogey and par competitions – Penalties as in match play.
Stableford competitions – see Note to Rule 32-1b.
c. Excess Club Declared Out of Play
Any club carried or used in breach of this Rule shall be declared out of play by the player immediately upon discovery that a breach has occurred and thereafter shall not be used by the player during the round.
PENALTY FOR BREACH OF RULE 4-4c: *Disqualification.*

RULE 5. THE BALL
5-1. General
The ball the player uses shall conform to requirements specified in Appendix III on maximum weight, minimum size, spherical symmetry, initial velocity and overall distance.
Note: The Committee may require, in the conditions of a competition (Rule 33-1), that the ball the player uses must be named on the current List of Conforming Golf Balls issued by the Royal and Ancient Golf Club of St. Andrews.

5-2. Foreign Material
Foreign material must not be applied to a ball for the purpose of changing its playing characteristics.
PENALTY FOR BREACH OF RULE 5-1 or 5-2: *Disqualification.*

5-3. Ball Unfit for Play
A ball is unfit for play if it is visibly cut, cracked or out of shape. A ball is not unfit for play solely because mud or other materials adhere to it, its surface is scratched or scraped or its paint is damaged or discoloured.

If a player has reason to believe his ball has become unfit for play during the play of the hole being played, he may during the play of such hole lift his ball without penalty to determine whether it is unfit.

Before lifting the ball, the player must announce his intention to his opponent in match play or his marker or a fellow-competitor in stroke play and mark the position of the ball. He may then lift and examine the ball without cleaning it and must give his opponent, marker or fellow-competitor an opportunity to examine the ball.

If he fails to comply with this procedure, *he shall incur a penalty of one stroke.*

If it is determined that the ball has become unfit for play during play of the hole being played, the player may substitute another ball, placing it on the spot where the original ball lay. Otherwise, the original ball shall be replaced.

If a ball breaks into pieces as a result of a stroke, the stroke shall be cancelled and the player shall play a ball without penalty as nearly as possible at the spot from which the original ball was played (see Rule 20-5):
PENALTY FOR BREACH OF RULE 5-3:
Match play – Loss of hole; Stroke play – Two strokes.
If a player incurs the general penalty for breach of Rule 5-3, no additional penalty under the Rule shall be applied.
Note: If the opponent, marker or fellow-competitor wishes to dispute a claim of unfitness, he must do so before the player plays another ball.
(Cleaning ball lifted from putting green or under any other Rule – see Rule 21.)

PLAYER'S RESPONSIBILITIES

RULE 6. THE PLAYER
Definition
A "marker" is one who is appointed by the Committee to record a competitor's score in stroke play. He may be a fellow-competitor. He is not a referee.
6-1. Conditions of Competition
The player is responsible for knowing the conditions under which the competition is to be played (Rule 33-1).
6-2. Handicap

a. Match Play

Before starting a match in a handicap competition, the players should determine from one another their respective handicaps. If a player begins the match having declared a higher handicap which would affect the number of strokes given or received, *he shall be disqualified;* otherwise, the player shall play off the declared handicap.

b. Stroke Play

In any round of a handicap competition, the competitor shall ensure that his handicap is recorded on his score card before it is returned to the Committee. If no handicap is recorded on his score card before it is returned, or if the recorded handicap is higher than that to which he is entitled and this affects the number of strokes received, *he shall be disqualified* from that round of the handicap competition; otherwise, the score shall stand.

Note: It is the player's responsibility to know the holes at which handicap strokes are to be given or received.

6-3. Time of Starting and Groups

a. Time of Starting

The player shall start at the time laid down by the Committee.

b. Groups

In stroke play, the competitor shall remain throughout the round in the group arranged by the Committee unless the Committee authorises or ratifies a change.

PENALTY FOR BREACH OF RULE 6-3:
Disqualification.

(Best-ball and four-ball play – see Rules 30-3a and 31-2.)

Note: The Committee may provide in the conditions of a competition (Rule 33-1) that, if the player arrives at his starting point, ready to play, within five minutes after his starting time, in the absence of circumstances which warrant waiving the penalty of disqualification as provided in Rule 33-7, the penalty for failure to start on time is *loss of the first hole in match play or two strokes at the first hole in stroke play* instead of disqualification.

6-4. Caddie

The player may have only one <u>caddie</u> at any one time, *under penalty of disqualification.*

For any breach of a Rule by his caddie, the player incurs the applicable penalty.

6-5. Ball

The responsibility for playing the proper ball rests with the player. Each player should put an identification mark on his ball.

6-6. Scoring in Stroke Play

a. Recording Scores

After each hole the <u>marker</u> should check the score with the competitor and record it. On completion of the round the marker shall sign the card and hand it to the competitor. If more than one marker records the scores, each shall sign for the part for which he is responsible.

b. Signing and Returning Card

After completion of the round, the competitor should check his score for each hole and settle any doubtful points with the Committee. He shall ensure that the marker has signed the card, countersign the card himself and return it to the Committee as soon as possible.

PENALTY FOR BREACH OF RULE 6-6b:
Disqualification.

c. Alteration of Card

No alteration may be made on a card after the competitor has returned it to the Committee.

d. Wrong Score for Hole

The competitor is responsible for the correctness of the score recorded for each hole on his card. If he returns a score for any hole lower than actually taken, *he shall be disqualified.* If he returns a score for any hole higher than actually taken, the score as returned shall stand.

Note 1: The Committee is responsible for the addition of scores and application of the handicap recorded on the card – see Rule 33-5.

Note 2: In four-ball stroke play, see also Rule 31-4 and -7a.

6-7. Undue Delay; Slow Play

The player shall play without undue delay and in accordance with any pace of play guidelines which may be laid down by the Committee. Between completion of a hole and playing from the next teeing ground, the player shall not unduly delay play.

PENALTY FOR BREACH OF RULE 6-7:
Match play – Loss of hole; Stroke play – Two strokes.
For subsequent offence – Disqualification.

Note 1: If the player unduly delays play between holes, he is delaying the play of the next hole and the penalty applies to that hole.

Note 2: For the purpose of preventing slow play, the Committee may, in the conditions of a competition (Rule 33-1), lay down pace of play guidelines including maximum periods of time allowed to complete a stipulated round, a hole or a stroke.

In stroke play only, the Committee may, in such a condition, modify the penalty for a breach of this Rule as follows:
First offence – One stroke;
Second offence – Two strokes.
For subsequent offence – Disqualification.

6-8. Discontinuance of Play

a. When Permitted

The player shall not discontinue play unless:
(i) the Committee has suspended play;
(ii) he believes there is danger from lightning;
(iii) he is seeking a decision from the Committee on a doubtful or disputed point (see Rules 2-5 and 34-3); or
(iv) there is some other good reason such as sudden illness.

Bad weather is not of itself a good reason for discontinuing play.

If the player discontinues play without specific permission from the Committee, he shall report to the Committee as soon as practicable. If he does so and the Committee considers his reason satisfactory, the player incurs no penalty. Otherwise, *the player shall be disqualified.*

Exception in match play: Players discontinuing match play by agreement are not subject to disqualification unless by so doing the competition is delayed.

Note: Leaving the course does not of itself constitute discontinuance of play.

b. Procedure When Play Suspended by Committee

When play is suspended by the Committee, if the players in a match or group are between the play of two holes, they shall not resume play until the Committee has ordered a resumption of play. If they are in the process of playing a hole, they may continue provided they do so without delay. If they choose to continue, they shall discontinue either before or immediately after completing the hole, and shall not thereafter resume play until the Committee has ordered a resumption of play.

When play has been suspended by the Committee, the player shall resume play when the Committee has ordered a resumption of play.

PENALTY FOR BREACH OF RULE 6-8b:
Disqualification.

Note: The Committee may provide in the conditions of a competition (Rule 33-1) that, in potentially dangerous situations, play shall be discontinued immediately following a suspension of play by the Committee. If a player fails to discontinue play immediately, *he shall be disqualified* unless circumstances warrant waiving such penalty as provided in Rule 33-7.

(Resumption of play – see Rule 33-2d.)

c. Lifting Ball When Play Discontinued

When during the play of a hole a player discontinues play under Rule 6-8a, he may lift his ball. A ball may be cleaned when so lifted. If a ball has been so lifted, the player shall, when play is resumed, place a ball on the spot from which the original ball was lifted.

PENALTY FOR BREACH OF RULE 6-8c:
Match play – Loss of hole; Stroke play – Two strokes.

RULE 7. PRACTICE

7-1. Before or Between Rounds

a. Match Play

On any day of a match play competition, a player may practise on the competition <u>course</u> before a round.

b. Stroke Play

On any day of a stroke competition or playoff, a competitor shall not practise on the competition <u>course</u> or test the surface of any putting green on the course before a round or play-off. When two or more rounds of a stroke competition are to be played over consecutive days, practice between those rounds on any competition course remaining to be played is prohibited.

Exception: Practice putting or chipping on or near the first <u>teeing ground</u> before starting a round or play-off is permitted.

PENALTY FOR BREACH OF RULE 7-1b:
Disqualification.

Note: The Committee may in the conditions of a competition (Rule 33-1) prohibit practice on the competition course on any day of a match play competition or permit practice on the competition course or part of the course (Rule 33-2c) on any day of or between rounds of a stroke competition.

7-2. During Round

A player shall not play a practice <u>stroke</u> either during the play of a hole or between the play of two holes except that, between the play of two holes, the player may practise putting or chipping on or near the <u>putting green</u> of the hole last played, any practice putting green or the <u>teeing ground</u> of the next hole to be played in the round, provided such practice stroke is not played from a hazard and does not unduly delay play (Rule 6-7).

Strokes played in continuing the play of a hole, the result of which has been decided, are not practice strokes.

Exception: When play has been suspended by the Committee, a player may, prior to resumption of play, practise (a) as provided in this Rule, (b) anywhere other than on the competition course and (c) as otherwise permitted by the Committee.

PENALTY FOR BREACH OF RULE 7-2:
Match play – Loss of hole; Stroke play – Two strokes.

In the event of a breach between the play of two holes, the penalty applies to the next hole.

Note 1: A practice swing is not a practice <u>stroke</u> and may be taken at any place, provided the player does not breach the Rules.

Note 2: The Committee may prohibit practice on or near the <u>putting green</u> of the hole last played.

RULE 8. ADVICE; INDICATING LINE OF PLAY

Definitions

"Advice" is any counsel or suggestion which could influence a player in determining his play, the choice of a club or the method of making a <u>stroke</u>.

Information on the Rules or on matters of public information, such as the position of hazards or the flagstick on the putting green, is not advice.

The "line of play" is the direction which the player wishes his ball to take after a stroke, plus a reasonable distance on either side of the intended direction. The line of play extends vertically upwards from the ground, but does not extend beyond the hole.

8-1. Advice

During a <u>stipulated round</u>, a player shall not give <u>advice</u> to anyone in the competition except his partner. A player may ask for advice during a stipulated round from only his partner or either of their caddies.

8-2. Indicating Line of Play

a. Other Than on Putting Green

Except on the <u>putting green</u>, a player may have the <u>line of play</u> indicated to him by anyone, but no one shall be positioned by the player on or close to the line or an extension of the line beyond the hole while the <u>stroke</u> is being played. Any mark placed during the play of a hole by the player or with his knowledge to indicate the line shall be removed before the stroke is played.

Exception: Flagstick attended or held up – see Rule 17-1.

b. On the Putting Green

When the player's ball is on the <u>putting green</u>, the player, his partner or either of their caddies may, before but not during the <u>stroke</u>, point out a line for putting, but in so doing the putting green shall not be touched. No mark shall be placed anywhere to indicate a line for putting.

PENALTY FOR BREACH OF RULE:
Match play – Loss of hole; Stroke play – Two strokes.

Note: The Committee may, in the conditions of a team competition (Rule 33-1), permit each team to appoint one person who may give <u>advice</u> (including pointing out a line for putting) to members of that team. The Committee may lay down conditions relating to the appointment and permitted conduct of such person, who must be identified to the Committee before giving advice.

RULE 9. INFORMATION AS TO STROKES TAKEN

9-1. General

The number of strokes a player has taken shall include any penalty strokes incurred.

9-2. Match Play

A player who has incurred a penalty shall inform his opponent as soon as practicable, unless he is obviously proceeding under a Rule involving a penalty and this has been observed by his opponent. If he

fails so to inform his opponent, he shall be deemed to have given wrong information, even if he was not aware that he had incurred a penalty.

An opponent is entitled to ascertain from the player, during the play of a hole, the number of strokes he has taken and, after play of a hole, the number of strokes taken on the hole just completed.

If during the play of a hole the player gives or is deemed to give wrong information as to the number of strokes taken, he shall incur no penalty if he corrects the mistake before his opponent has played his next stroke. If the player fails so to correct the wrong information, *he shall lose the hole*.

If after play of a hole the player gives or is deemed to give wrong information as to the number of strokes taken on the hole just completed and this affects the opponent's understanding of the result of the hole, he shall incur no penalty if he corrects his mistake before any player plays from the next <u>teeing ground</u> or, in the case of the last hole of the match, before all players leave the <u>putting green</u>. If the player fails so to correct the wrong information, *he shall lose the hole*.

9-3. Stroke Play

A competitor who has incurred a penalty should inform his marker as soon as practicable.

ORDER OF PLAY

RULE 10. ORDER OF PLAY

10-1. Match Play

a. Teeing Ground

The side entitled to play first from the <u>teeing ground</u> is said to have the "honour".

The side which shall have the honour at the first teeing ground shall be determined by the order of the draw. In the absence of a draw, the honour should be decided by lot.

The side which wins a hole shall take the honour at the next teeing ground. If a hole has been halved, the side which had the honour at the previous teeing ground shall retain it.

b. Other Than on Teeing Ground

When the balls are in play, the ball farther from the hole shall be played first. If the balls are equidistant from the hole, the ball to be played first should be decided by lot.

Exception: Rule 30-3c (best-ball and four-ball match play).

c. Playing Out of Turn

If a player plays when his opponent should have played, the opponent may immediately require the player to cancel the stroke so played and, in correct order, play a ball without penalty as nearly as possible at the spot from which the original ball was last played (see Rule 20-5).

10-2. Stroke Play

a. Teeing Ground

The competitor entitled to play first from the <u>teeing ground</u> is said to have the "honour".

The competitor who shall have the honour at the first teeing ground shall be determined by the order of the draw. In the absence of a draw, the honour should be decided by lot.

The competitor with the lowest score at a hole shall take the honour at the next teeing ground. The competitor with the second lowest score shall play next and so

on. If two or more competitors have the same score at a hole, they shall play from the next teeing ground in the same order as at the previous teeing ground.

b. Other Than on Teeing Ground

When the balls are in play, the ball farthest from the hole shall be played first. If two or more balls are equidistant from the hole, the ball to be played first should be decided by lot.

Exceptions: Rules 22 (ball interfering with or assisting play) and 31-5 (four-ball stroke play).

c. Playing Out of Turn

If a competitor plays out of turn, no penalty is incurred and the ball shall be played as it lies. If, however, the Committee determines that competitors have agreed to play in an order other than that set forth in Clauses 2a and 2b of this Rule to give one of them an advantage, *they shall be disqualified*.

(Incorrect order of play in threesomes and foursomes stroke play — see Rule 29-3.)

10-3. Provisional Ball or Second Ball from Teeing Ground

If a player plays a <u>provisional ball</u> or a second ball from a <u>teeing ground</u>, he should do so after his opponent or fellow-competitor has played his first <u>stroke</u>. If a player plays a provisional ball or a second ball out of turn, Clauses 1c and 2c of this Rule shall apply.

10-4. Ball Moved in Measuring

If a ball is moved in measuring to determine which ball is farther from the hole, no penalty is incurred and the ball shall be replaced.

TEEING GROUND

RULE 11. TEEING GROUND

Definition

The "teeing ground" is the starting place for the hole to be played. It is a rectangular area two club-lengths in depth, the front and the sides of which are defined by the outside limits of two tee-markers. A ball is outside the teeing ground when all of it lies outside the teeing ground.

11-1. Teeing

In teeing, the ball may be placed on the ground, on an irregularity of surface created by the player on the ground or on a tee, sand or other substance in order to raise it off the ground.

A player may stand outside the <u>teeing ground</u> to play a ball within it.

11-2. Tee-Markers

Before a player plays his first stroke with any ball from the teeing ground of the hole being played, the tee-markers are deemed to be fixed. In such circumstances, if the player moves or allows to be moved a tee-marker for the purpose of avoiding interference with his stance, the area of his intended swing or his line of play, *he shall incur the penalty for a breach of Rule 13-2*.

11-3. Ball Falling Off Tee

If a ball, when not <u>in play</u>, falls off a tee or is knocked off a tee by the player in addressing it, it may be re-teed without penalty, but if a <u>stroke</u> is made at the ball in these circumstances, whether the ball is moving or not, the stroke counts but no penalty is incurred.

11-4. Playing from Outside Teeing Ground

a. Match Play

If a player, when starting a hole, plays a ball from outside the <u>teeing ground</u>, the opponent may immediately require the player to cancel the stroke so played and play a ball from within the teeing ground, without penalty.

b. Stroke Play

If a competitor, when starting a hole, plays a ball from outside the <u>teeing ground</u>, *he shall incur a penalty of two strokes* and shall then play a ball from within the teeing ground.

If the competitor plays a stroke from the next teeing ground without first correcting his mistake or, in the case of the last hole of the round, leaves the <u>putting green</u> without first declaring his intention to correct his mistake, *he shall be disqualified*.

Strokes played by a competitor from outside the teeing ground do not count in his score.

11-5. Playing from Wrong Teeing Ground

The provisions of Rule 11-4 apply.

PLAYING THE BALL

RULE 12. SEARCHING FOR AND IDENTIFYING BALL

Definitions

A "hazard" is any <u>bunker</u> or <u>water hazard</u>.

A "bunker" is a <u>hazard</u> consisting of a prepared area of ground, often a hollow, from which turf or soil has been removed and replaced with sand or the like. Grass-covered ground bordering or within a bunker is not part of the bunker. The margin of a bunker extends vertically downwards, but not upwards. A ball is in a bunker when it lies in or any part of it touches the bunker.

A "water hazard" is any sea, lake, pond, river, ditch, surface drainage ditch or other open water course (whether or not containing water) and anything of a similar nature.

All ground or water within the margin of a water hazard is part of the water hazard. The margin of a water hazard extends vertically upwards and downwards. Stakes and lines defining the margins of water hazards are in the hazards. Such stakes are obstructions. A ball is in a water hazard when it lies in or any part of it touches the water hazard.

12-1. Searching for Ball; Seeing Ball

In searching for his ball anywhere on the course, the player may touch or bend long grass, rushes, bushes, whins, heather or the like, but only to the extent necessary to find and identify it, provided that this does not improve the lie of the ball, the area of his intended swing or his line of play.

A player is not necessarily entitled to see his ball when playing a stroke.

In a <u>hazard</u>, if a ball is covered by <u>loose impediments</u> or sand, the player may remove by probing, raking or other means as much thereof as will enable him to see a part of the ball. If an excess is removed, no penalty is incurred and the ball shall be recovered so that only a part of the ball is visible. If the ball is moved in such removal, no penalty is incurred; the ball shall be replaced and, if necessary, re-covered. As to removal of loose impediments outside a hazard, see Rule 23.

If a ball lying in <u>casual water</u>, <u>ground under repair</u> or a hole, cast or runway

made by a burrowing animal, a reptile or a bird is accidentally moved during search, no penalty is incurred; the ball shall be replaced, unless the player elects to proceed under Rule 25-1b.

If a ball is believed to be lying in water in a <u>water hazard</u>, the player may probe for it with a club or otherwise. If the ball is moved in so doing, no penalty is incurred; the ball shall be replaced, unless the player elects to proceed under Rule 26-1.

PENALTY FOR BREACH OF RULE 12-1:

Match play – Loss of hole; Stroke play – Two strokes.

12-2. Identifying Ball

The responsibility for playing the proper ball rests with the player. Each player should put an identification mark on his ball.

Except in a <u>hazard</u>, the player may, without penalty, lift a ball he believes to be his own for the purpose of identification and clean it to the extent necessary for identification. If the ball is the player's ball, he shall replace it. Before lifting the ball, the player must announce his intention to his opponent in match play or his marker or a fellow-competitor in stroke play and mark the position of the ball. He must then give his opponent, marker or fellow-competitor an opportunity to observe the lifting and replacement. If he lifts his ball without announcing his intention in advance, marking the position of the ball or giving his opponent, marker or fellow-competitor an opportunity to observe, or if he lifts his ball for identification in a hazard, or cleans it more than necessary for identification, *he shall incur a penalty of one stroke* and the ball shall be replaced.

If a player who is required to replace a ball fails to do so, *he shall incur the penalty* for a breach of Rule 20-3a, but no additional penalty under Rule 12-2 shall be applied.

RULE 13. BALL PLAYED AS IT LIES; LIE, AREA OF INTENDED SWING AND LINE OF PLAY; STANCE

Definitions

A "hazard" is any <u>bunker</u> or <u>water hazard</u>.

A "bunker" is a <u>hazard</u> consisting of a prepared area of ground, often a hollow, from which turf or soil has been removed and replaced with sand or the like. Grass-covered ground bordering or within a bunker is not part of the bunker. The margin of a bunker extends vertically downwards, but not upwards. A ball is in a bunker when it lies in or any part of it touches the bunker.

A "water hazard" is any sea, lake, pond, river, ditch, surface drainage ditch or other open water course (whether or not containing water) and anything of a similar nature.

All ground or water within the margin of a water hazard is part of the water hazard. The margin of a water hazard extends vertically upwards and downwards. Stakes and lines defining the margins of water hazards are in the hazards. Such stakes are obstructions. A ball is in a water hazard when it lies in or any part of it touches the water hazard.

The "line of play" is the direction which the player wishes his ball to take after a stroke, plus a reasonable distance on either side of the intended direction.

The line of play extends vertically upwards from the ground, but does not extend beyond the hole.

13-1. Ball Played as It Lies
The ball shall be played as it lies, except as otherwise provided in the Rules. (Ball at rest moved – see Rule 18.)

13-2. Improving Lie, Area of Intended Swing or Line of Play
Except as provided in the Rules, a player shall not improve or allow to be improved:

the position or lie of his ball,

the area of his intended swing,

his line of play or a reasonable extension of that line beyond the hole or

the area in which he is to drop or place a ball by any of the following actions:

moving, bending or breaking anything growing or fixed (including immovable obstructions and objects defining out of bounds) or

removing or pressing down sand, loose soil, replaced divots, other cut turf placed in position or other irregularities of surface

except as follows:

as may occur in fairly taking his stance,

in making a stroke or the backward movement of his club for a stroke,

on the teeing ground in creating or eliminating irregularities of surface, or

on the putting green in removing sand and loose soil as provided in Rule 16-1a or in repairing damage as provided in Rule 16-1c.

The club may be grounded only lightly and shall not be pressed on the ground. *Exception:* Ball in hazard – see Rule 13-4.

13-3. Building Stance
A player is entitled to place his feet firmly in taking his stance, but he shall not build a stance.

13-4. Ball in Hazard
Except as provided in the Rules, before making a stroke at a ball which is in a hazard (whether a bunker or a water hazard) or which, having been lifted from a hazard, may be dropped or placed in the hazard, the player shall not:

a. Test the condition of the hazard or any similar hazard,

b. Touch the ground in the hazard or water in the water hazard with a club or otherwise, or

c. Touch or move a loose impediment lying in or touching the hazard.

Exceptions:

1. Provided nothing is done which constitutes testing the condition of the hazard or improves the lie of the ball, there is no penalty if the player (a) touches the ground in any hazard or water in a water hazard as a result of or to prevent falling, in removing an obstruction, in measuring or in retrieving or lifting a ball under any Rule or (b) places his clubs in a hazard.

2. The player after playing the stroke, or his caddie at any time without the authority of the player, may smooth sand or soil in the hazard, provided that, if the ball is still in the hazard, nothing is done which improves the lie of the ball or assists the player in his subsequent play of the hole.

Note: At any time, including at address or in the backward movement for the stroke, the player may touch with a club or otherwise any obstruction, any construction declared by the Committee to be an integral part of the course or any grass, bush, tree or other growing thing.

PENALTY FOR BREACH OF RULE:

Match play – Loss of hole; Stroke play – Two strokes.

(Searching for ball – see Rule 12-1.)

RULE 14. STRIKING THE BALL
Definition
A "stroke" is the forward movement of the club made with the intention of fairly striking at and moving the ball, but if a player checks his downswing voluntarily before the clubhead reaches the ball he is deemed not to have made a stroke.

14-1. Ball to be Fairly Struck at
The ball shall be fairly struck at with the head of the club and must not be pushed, scraped or spooned.

14-2. Assistance
In making a stroke, a player shall not accept physical assistance or protection from the elements.

PENALTY FOR BREACH OF RULE 14-1 or -2: *Match play – Loss of hole; Stroke play – Two strokes.*

14-3. Artificial Devices and Unusual Equipment
A player in doubt as to whether use of an item would constitute a breach of Rule 14-3 should consult the Royal and Ancient Golf Club of St. Andrews.

A manufacturer may submit to the Royal and Ancient Golf Club of St. Andrews a sample of an item which is to be manufactured for a ruling as to whether its use during a stipulated round would cause a player to be in breach of Rule 14-3. Such sample will become the property of the Royal and Ancient Golf Club of St. Andrews for reference purposes. If a manufacturer fails to submit a sample before manufacturing and/or marketing the item, he assumes the risk of a ruling that use of the item would be contrary to the Rules of Golf.

Except as provided in the Rules, during a stipulated round the player shall not use any artificial device or unusual equipment:

a. Which might assist him in making a stroke or in his play; or

b. For the purpose of gauging or measuring distance or conditions which might affect his play; or

c. Which might assist him in gripping the club, except that:

(i)   plain gloves may be worn;

(ii)   resin, powder and drying or moisturising agents may be used;

(iii)   tape or gauze may be applied to the grip (provided such application does not render the grip non-conforming under Rule 4-1c); and

(iv)   a towel or handkerchief may be wrapped around the grip.

PENALTY FOR BREACH OF RULE 14-3: *Disqualification.*

14-4. Striking the Ball More than Once
If a player's club strikes the ball more than once in the course of a stroke, the player shall count the stroke and add a penalty stroke, making two strokes in all.

14-5. Playing Moving Ball
A player shall not play while his ball is moving.

Exceptions:

Ball falling off tee – Rule 11-3.

Striking the ball more than once – Rule 14-4.

Ball moving in water – Rule 14-6.

When the ball begins to move only after the player has begun the stroke or the backward movement of his club for the stroke, he shall incur no penalty under this Rule for playing a moving ball, but he is not exempt from any penalty incurred under the following Rules:

Ball at rest moved by player — Rule 18-2a.

Ball at rest moving after address — Rule 18-2b.

Ball at rest moving after loose impediment touched– Rule 18-2c.

(Ball purposely deflected or stopped by player, partner or caddie – see Rule 1-2).

14-6. Ball Moving in Water
When a ball is moving in water in a water hazard, the player may, without penalty, make a stroke, but he must not delay making his stroke in order to allow the wind or current to improve the position of the ball. A ball moving in water in a water hazard may be lifted if the player elects to invoke Rule 26.

PENALTY FOR BREACH OF RULE 14-5 or -6 *Match play – Loss of hole; Stroke play – Two strokes.*

RULE 15. WRONG BALL; SUBSTITUTED BALL
Definition
A "wrong ball" is any ball other than the player's:

a. Ball in play,

b. Provisional ball, or

c. Second ball played under Rule 3-3 or Rule 20-7b in stroke play.

Note: Ball in play includes a ball substituted for the ball in play whether or not such substitution is permitted.

15-1. General
A player must hole out with the ball played from the teeing ground unless a Rule permits him to substitute another ball. If a player substitutes another ball when not so permitted, that ball is not a wrong ball; it becomes the ball in play and, if the error is not corrected as provided in Rule 20-6, *the player shall incur a penalty of loss of hole in match play or two strokes in stroke play.*

(Playing from wrong place – see Rule 20-7).

15-2. Match Play
If a player plays a stroke with a wrong ball except in a hazard, *he shall lose the hole.*

If a player plays any strokes in a hazard with a wrong ball, there is no penalty. Strokes played in a hazard with a wrong ball do not count in the player's score. If the wrong ball belongs to another player, its owner shall place a ball on the spot from which the wrong ball was first played.

If the player and opponent exchange balls during the play of a hole, the first to play the wrong ball other than from a hazard shall lose the hole; when this cannot be determined, the hole shall be played out with the balls exchanged.

15-3. Stroke Play
If a competitor plays a stroke or strokes with a wrong ball, *he shall incur a penalty of two strokes,* unless the only stroke or strokes played with such ball were played when it was in a hazard, in which case no penalty is incurred.

The competitor must correct his mistake by playing the correct ball. If he fails to correct his mistake before he plays a stroke from the next teeing ground or, in the case of the last hole of the round, fails to declare his intention to correct his mistake before leaving the putting green, *he shall be disqualified.*

Strokes played by a competitor with a wrong ball do not count in his score.

If the wrong ball belongs to another competitor, its owner shall place a ball on the spot from which the wrong ball was first played.

(Lie of ball to be placed or replaced altered – see Rule 20-3b.)

THE PUTTING GREEN

RULE 16. THE PUTTING GREEN
Definitions
The "putting green" is all ground of the hole being played which is specially prepared for putting or otherwise defined as such by the Committee. A ball is on the putting green when any part of it touches the putting green.

The "line of putt" is the line which the player wishes his ball to take after a stroke on the putting green. Except with respect to Rule 16-1e, the line of putt includes a reasonable distance on either side of the intended line. The line of putt does not extend beyond the hole.

A ball is "holed" when it is at rest within the circumference of the hole and all of it is below the level of the lip of the hole.

16-1. General
a. Touching Line of Putt
The line of putt must not be touched except:

(i)   the player may move sand and loose soil on the putting green and other loose impediments by picking them up or by brushing them aside with his hand or a club without pressing anything down;

(ii)   in addressing the ball, the player may place the club in front of the ball without pressing anything down;

(iii)   in measuring – Rule 10-4;

(iv)   in lifting the ball – Rule 16-1b;

(v)   in pressing down a ball-marker;

(vi)   in repairing old hole plugs or ball marks on the putting green – Rule 16-1c; and

(vii)   in removing movable obstructions – Rule 24-1.

(Indicating line for putting on putting green – See Rule 8-2b.)

b. Lifting Ball
A ball on the putting green may be lifted and, if desired, cleaned. A ball so lifted shall be replaced on the spot from which it was lifted.

c. Repair of Hole Plugs, Ball Marks and Other Damage
The player may repair an old hole plug or damage to the putting green caused by the impact of a ball, whether or not the player's ball lies on the putting green. If the ball is moved in the process of such repair, it shall be replaced, without penalty. Any other damage to the putting green shall not be repaired if it might assist the player in his subsequent play of the hole.

d. Testing Surface
During the play of a hole, a player shall not test the surface of the putting green by rolling a ball or roughening or scraping the surface.

e. Standing Astride or on Line of Putt
The player shall not make a stroke on the putting green from a stance astride, or with either foot touching, the line of putt or an extension of that line behind the ball.

f. Position of Caddie or Partner
While making a stroke on the putting green, the player shall not allow his caddie,

his partner or his partner's caddie to position himself on or close to an extension of the line of putt behind the ball.

g. Playing Stroke While Another Ball in Motion

The player shall not play a stroke while another ball is in motion after a stroke from the putting green, except that, if a player does so, he incurs no penalty if it was his turn to play.

(Lifting ball interfering with or assisting play while another ball in motion – see Rule 22.)

PENALTY FOR BREACH OF RULE 16-1: *Match play – Loss of hole; Stroke play – Two strokes.*

16-2. Ball Overhanging Hole

When any part of the ball overhangs the lip of the hole, the player is allowed enough time to reach the hole without unreasonable delay and an additional ten seconds to determine whether the ball is at rest. If by then the ball has not fallen into the hole, it is deemed to be at rest. If the ball subsequently falls into the hole, the player is deemed to have holed out with his last stroke, and *he shall add a penalty stroke to his score* for the hole; otherwise there is no penalty under this Rule.

(Undue delay – see Rule 6-7.)

RULE 17. THE FLAGSTICK

17-1. Flagstick Attended, Removed or Held Up

Before and during the stroke, the player may have the flagstick attended, removed or held up to indicate the position of the hole. This may be done only on the authority of the player before he plays his stroke.

If, prior to the stroke, the flagstick is attended, removed or held up by anyone with the player's knowledge and no objection is made, the player shall be deemed to have authorised it. If anyone attends or holds up the flagstick or stands near the hole while a stroke is being played, he shall be deemed to be attending the flagstick until the ball comes to rest.

17-2. Unauthorised Attendance

a. Match Play

In match play, an opponent or his caddie shall not, without the authority or prior knowledge of the player, attend, remove or hold up the flagstick while the player is making a stroke or his ball is in motion.

b. Stroke Play

In stroke play, if a fellow-competitor or his caddie attends, removes or holds up the flagstick without the competitor's authority or prior knowledge while the competitor is making a stroke or his ball is in motion, *the fellow-competitor shall incur the penalty* for breach of this Rule. In such circumstances, if the competitor's ball strikes the flagstick, the person attending it or anything carried by him, the competitor incurs no penalty and the ball shall be played as it lies, except that, if the stroke was played from the putting green, the stroke shall be cancelled, the ball replaced and the stroke replayed.

PENALTY FOR BREACH OF RULE 17-1 or -2: *Match play – Loss of hole; Stroke play – Two strokes.*

17-3. Ball Striking Flagstick or Attendant

The player's ball shall not strike:

a. The flagstick when attended, removed or held up by the player, his partner or either of their caddies, or by another person with the player's authority or prior knowledge; or

b. The player's caddie, his partner or his partner's caddie when attending the flagstick, or another person attending the flagstick with the player's authority or prior knowledge or anything carried by any such person; or

c. The flagstick in the hole, unattended, when the ball has been played from the putting green.

PENALTY FOR BREACH OF RULE 17-3: *Match play – Loss of hole; Stroke play – Two strokes, and the ball shall be played as it lies.*

17-4. Ball Resting Against Flagstick

If the ball rests against the flagstick when it is in the hole, the player or another person authorised by him may move or remove the flagstick and if the ball falls into the hole, the player shall be deemed to have holed out with his last stroke; otherwise the ball, if moved, shall be placed on the lip of the hole, without penalty.

BALL MOVED, DEFLECTED OR STOPPED

RULE 18. BALL AT REST MOVED
Definitions

A ball is deemed to have "moved" if it leaves its position and comes to rest in any other place.

An "outside agency" is any agency not part of the match or, in stroke play, not part of the competitor's side, and includes a referee, a marker, an observer and a forecaddie. Neither wind nor water is an outside agency.

"Equipment" is anything used, worn or carried by or for the player except any ball he has played at the hole being played and any small object, such as a coin or a tee, when used to mark the position of a ball or the extent of an area in which a ball is to be dropped. Equipment includes a golf cart, whether or not motorised. If such a cart is shared by two or more players, the cart and everything in it are deemed to be the equipment of the player whose ball is involved except that, when the cart is being moved by one of the players sharing it, the cart and everything in it are deemed to be that player's equipment.

Note: A ball played at the hole being played is equipment when it has been lifted and not put back into play.

A player has "addressed the ball" when he has taken his stance and has also grounded his club, except that in a hazard a player has addressed the ball when he has taken his stance.

Taking the "stance" consists in a player placing his feet in position for and preparatory to making a stroke.

18-1. By Outside Agency

If a ball at rest is moved by an outside agency, the player shall incur no penalty and the ball shall be replaced before the player plays another stroke.

(Player's ball at rest moved by another ball – see Rule 18-5.)

18-2. By Player, Partner, Caddie or Equipment

a. General

When a player's ball is in play, if:

(i) the player, his partner or either of their caddies lifts or moves it, touches it purposely (except with a club in the act of addressing it) or causes it to move except as permitted by a Rule, or

(ii) equipment of the player or his partner causes the ball to move, *the player shall*

incur a penalty stroke. The ball shall be replaced unless the movement of the ball occurs after the player has begun his swing and he does not discontinue his swing.

Under the Rules no penalty is incurred if a player accidentally causes his ball to move in the following circumstances:

In measuring to determine which ball farther from hole – Rule 10-4

In searching for covered ball in hazard or for ball in casual water, ground under repair, etc. – Rule 12-1

In the process of repairing hole plug or ball mark – Rule 16-1c

In the process of removing loose impediment on putting green – Rule 18-2c

In the process of lifting ball under a Rule – Rule 20-1

In the process of placing or replacing ball under a Rule – Rule 20-3a

In removal of movable obstruction – Rule 24-1.

b. Ball Moving After Address

If a player's ball in play moves after he has addressed it (other than as a result of a stroke), the player shall be deemed to have moved the ball and *incur a penalty stroke.* The player shall replace the ball unless the movement of the ball occurs after he has begun his swing and he does not discontinue his swing.

c. Ball Moving After Loose Impediment Touched

Through the green, if the ball moves after any loose impediment lying within a club-length of it has been touched by the player, his partner or either of their caddies and before the player has addressed it, the player shall be deemed to have moved the ball and *shall incur a penalty stroke.* The player shall replace the ball unless the movement of the ball occurs after he has begun his swing and he does not discontinue his swing.

On the putting green, if the ball or the ball-marker moves in the process of removing any loose impediment, the ball or the ball-marker shall be replaced. There is no penalty provided the movement of the ball or the ball-marker is directly attributable to the removal of the loose impediment. Otherwise, *the player shall incur a penalty stroke* under Rule 18-2a or 20-1.

18-3. By Opponent, Caddie or Equipment in Match Play

a. During Search

If, during search for a player's ball, the ball is moved by an opponent, his caddie or his equipment, no penalty is incurred and the player shall replace the ball.

b. Other Than During Search

If, other than during search for a ball, the ball is touched or moved by an opponent, his caddie or his equipment, except as otherwise provided in the Rules, *the opponent shall incur a penalty stroke.* The player shall replace the ball.

(Ball moved in measuring to determine which ball farther from the hole – see Rule 10-4.)

(Playing a wrong ball – see Rule 15-2.)

18-4. By Fellow-Competitor, Caddie or Equipment in Stroke Play

If a competitor's ball is moved by a fellow-competitor, his caddie or his equipment, no penalty is incurred. The competitor shall replace his ball.

(Playing a wrong ball – see Rule 15-3.)

18-5. By Another Ball

If a ball in play and at rest is moved by

another ball in motion after a stroke, the moved ball shall be replaced.

PENALTY FOR BREACH OF RULE: Match play – Loss of hole; Stroke play – Two strokes.

If a player who is required to replace a ball fails to do so, he shall incur the general penalty for breach of Rule 18 but no additional penalty under Rule 18 shall be applied.

Note 1: If a ball to be replaced under this Rule is not immediately recoverable, another ball may be substituted.

Note 2: If it is impossible to determine the spot on which a ball is to be placed, see Rule 20-3c.

RULE 19. BALL IN MOTION DEFLECTED OR STOPPED
Definitions

An "outside agency" is any agency not part of the match or, in stroke play, not part of the competitor's side, and includes a referee, a marker, an observer and a forecaddie. Neither wind nor water is an outside agency.

"Equipment" is anything used, worn or carried by or for the player except any ball he has played at the hole being played and any small object, such as a coin or a tee, when used to mark the position of a ball or the extent of an area in which a ball is to be dropped. Equipment includes a golf cart, whether or not motorised. If such a cart is shared by two or more players, the cart and everything in it are deemed to be the equipment of the player whose ball is involved except that, when the cart is being moved by one of the players sharing it, the cart and everything in it are deemed to be that player's equipment.

Note: A ball played at the hole being played is equipment when it has been lifted and not put back into play.

19-1. By Outside Agency

If a ball in motion is accidentally deflected or stopped by any outside agency, it is a rub of the green, no penalty is incurred and the ball shall be played as it lies except:

a. If a ball in motion after a stroke other than on the putting green comes to rest in or on any moving or animate outside agency, the player shall, through the green or in a hazard, drop the ball, or on the putting green place the ball, as near as possible to the spot where the outside agency was when the ball came to rest in or on it, and

b. If a ball in motion after a stroke on the putting green is deflected or stopped by, or comes to rest in or on, any moving or animate outside agency except a worm or an insect, the stroke shall be cancelled, the ball replaced and the stroke replayed.

If the ball is not immediately recoverable, another ball may be substituted.

(Player's ball deflected or stopped by another ball – see Rule 19-5.)

Note: If the referee or the Committee determines that a player's ball has been purposely deflected or stopped by an outside agency, Rule 1-4 applies to the player. If the outside agency is a fellow-competitor or his caddie, Rule 1-2 applies to the fellow-competitor.

19-2. By Player, Partner, Caddie or Equipment

a. Match Play

If a player's ball is accidentally deflected or stopped by himself, his partner or

either of their caddies or equipment, *he shall lose the hole.*

b. Stroke Play

If a competitor's ball is accidentally deflected or stopped by himself, his partner or either of their caddies or equipment, *the competitor shall incur a penalty of two strokes.*The ball shall be played as it lies, except when it comes to rest in or on the competitor's, his partner's or either of their caddies' clothes or equipment, in which case the competitor shall through the green or in a hazard drop the ball, or on the putting green place the ball, as near as possible to where the article was when the ball came to rest in or on it.

Exception: Dropped Ball – see Rule 20-2a.

(Ball purposely deflected or stopped by player, partner or caddie – see Rule 1-2.)

19-3. By Opponent, Caddie or Equipment in Match Play

If a player's ball is accidentally deflected or stopped by an opponent, his caddie or his equipment, no penalty is incurred. The player may play the ball as it lies or, before another stroke is played by either side, cancel the stroke and play a ball without penalty as nearly as possible at the spot from which the original ball was last played (see Rule 20-5).

If the ball has come to rest in or on the opponent's or his caddie's clothes or equipment, the player may through the green or in a hazard drop the ball, or on the putting green place the ball, as near as possible to where the article was when the ball came to rest in or on it.

Exception: Ball striking person attending flagstick – see Rule 17-3b.

(Ball purposely deflected or stopped by opponent or caddie – see Rule 1-2.)

19-4. By Fellow-Competitor, Caddie or Equipment in Stroke Play

See Rule 19-1 regarding ball deflected by outside agency.

19-5. By Another Ball

a. At Rest

If a player's ball in motion after a stroke is deflected or stopped by a ball in play and at rest, the player shall play his ball as it lies.

In match play, no penalty is incurred. In stroke play, there is no penalty unless both balls lay on the putting green prior to the stroke, in which case *the player incurs a penalty of two strokes.*

b. In Motion

If a player's ball in motion after a stroke is deflected or stopped by another ball in motion after a stroke, the player shall play his ball as it lies. There is no penalty unless the player was in breach of Rule 16-1g, in which case *he shall incur the penalty for breach of that Rule.*

Exception: If the player's ball is in motion after a stroke on the putting green and the other ball in motion is an outside agency – see Rule 19-1b.

PENALTY FOR BREACH OF RULE: *Match play – Loss of hole; Stroke play – Two strokes.*

RELIEF SITUATIONS AND PROCEDURE

RULE 20. LIFTING, DROPPING AND PLACING; PLAYING FROM WRONG PLACE

20-1. Lifting

A ball to be lifted under the Rules may be lifted by the player, his partner or another person authorised by the player. In any such case, the player shall be responsible for any breach of the Rules.

The position of the ball shall be marked before it is lifted under a Rule which requires it to be replaced. If it is not marked, *the player shall incur a penalty of one stroke* and the ball shall be replaced. If it is not replaced, *the player shall incur the general penalty* for breach of this Rule but no additional penalty under Rule 20-1 shall be applied.

If a ball or ball-marker is accidentally moved in the process of lifting the ball under a Rule or marking its position, the ball or the ball-marker shall be replaced. There is no penalty provided the movement of the ball or the ball-marker is directly attributable to the specific act of marking the position of or lifting the ball. Otherwise, *the player shall incur a penalty stroke* under this Rule or Rule 18-2a.

Exception: If a player incurs a penalty for failing to act in accordance with Rule 5-3 or 12-2, no additional penalty under Rule 20-1 shall be applied.

Note: The position of a ball to be lifted should be marked by placing a ball-marker, a small coin or other similar object immediately behind the ball. If the ball-marker interferes with the play, stance, or stroke of another player, it should be placed one or more clubhead-lengths to one side

20-2. Dropping and Re-Dropping

a. By Whom and How

A ball to be dropped under the Rules shall be dropped by the player himself. He shall stand erect, hold the ball at shoulder height and arm's length and drop it. If a ball is dropped by any other person or in any other manner and the error is not corrected as provided in Rule 20-6, *the player shall incur a penalty stroke.*

If the ball touches the player, his partner, either of their caddies or their equipment before or after it strikes a part of the course, the ball shall be re-dropped, without penalty. There is no limit to the number of times a ball shall be re-dropped in such circumstances.

(Taking action to influence position or movement of ball – see Rule 1-2.)

b. Where to Drop

When a ball is to be dropped as near as possible to a specific spot, it shall be dropped not nearer the hole than the specific spot which, if it is not precisely known to the player, shall be estimated.

A ball when dropped must first strike a part of the course where the applicable Rule requires it to be dropped. If it is not so dropped, Rules 20-6 and -7 apply.

c. When to Re-Drop

A dropped ball shall be re-dropped without penalty if it:

(i)   rolls into a hazard;
(ii)   rolls out of a hazard;
(iii)   rolls onto a putting green;
(iv)   rolls out of bounds;
(v)   rolls to a position where there is interference by the condition from which relief was taken under Rule 24-2 (immovable obstruction) or Rule 25-1 (abnormal ground conditions), or rolls back into the pitch-mark from which it was lifted under Rule 25-2 (embedded ball);
(vi)   rolls and comes to rest more than two club-lengths from where it first struck a part of the course; or

(vii)   rolls and comes to rest nearer the hole than its original position or estimated position (see Rule 20-2b) unless otherwise permitted by the Rules.

(viii) rolls and comes to rest nearer the hole than the point where the original ball last crossed the margin of the area or hazard, (Rule 25-1c(i) and (ii)) or the margin of the water hazard (Rule 26-1b) or lateral water hazard (Rule 26-1c).

If the ball when re-dropped rolls into any position listed above, it shall be placed as near as possible to the spot where it first struck a part of the course when re-dropped.

If a ball to be re-dropped or placed under this Rule is not immediately recoverable, another ball may be substituted.

20-3. Placing and Replacing

a. By Whom and Where

A ball to be placed under the Rules shall be placed by the player or his partner. If a ball is to be replaced, the player, his partner or the person who lifted or moved it shall place it on the spot from which it was lifted or moved. In any such case, the player shall be responsible for any breach of the Rules.

If a ball or ball-marker is accidentally moved in the process of placing or replacing the ball, the ball or the ball-marker shall be replaced. There is no penalty provided the movement of the ball or the ball-marker is directly attributable to the specific act of placing or replacing the ball or removing the ball-marker. Otherwise, *the player shall incur a penalty stroke* under Rule 18-2a or 20-1.

b. Lie of Ball to Be Placed or Replaced Altered

If the original lie of a ball to be placed or replaced has been altered:

(i)   except in a hazard, the ball shall be placed in the nearest lie most similar to the original lie which is not more than one club-length from the original lie, not nearer the hole and not in a hazard;

(ii) in a water hazard, the ball shall be placed in accordance with Clause (i) above, except that the ball must be placed in the water hazard;

(iii) in a bunker, the original lie shall be recreated as nearly as possible and the ball shall be placed in that lie.

c. Spot Not Determinable

If it is impossible to determine the spot where the ball is to be placed or replaced:

(i)   through the green, the ball shall be dropped as near as possible to the place where it lay but not in a hazard or on a putting green;

(ii) in a hazard, the ball shall be dropped in the hazard as near as possible to the place where it lay;

(iii) on the putting green, the ball shall be placed as near as possible to the place where it lay but not in a hazard.

d. Ball Fails to Come to Rest on Spot

If a ball when placed fails to come to rest on the spot on which it was placed, it shall be replaced without penalty. If it still fails to come to rest on that spot:

(i)   except in a hazard, it shall be placed at the nearest spot not nearer the hole or in a hazard where it can be placed at rest;

(ii)   in a hazard, it shall be placed in the hazard at the nearest spot not nearer the hole where it can be placed at rest.

If a ball when placed comes to rest on the spot on which it is placed, and it subsequently moves, there is no penalty and the ball shall be played as it lies, unless the provisions of any other Rule apply.

PENALTY FOR BREACH OF RULE 20-1, -2 or -3: *Match play – Loss of hole; Stroke play – Two strokes.*

20-4. When Ball Dropped or Placed Is in Play

If the player's ball in play has been lifted, it is again in play when dropped or placed.

A substituted ball becomes the ball in play when it has been dropped or placed.

(Ball incorrectly substituted – see Rule 15-1.)

(Lifting ball incorrectly substituted, dropped or placed – see Rule 20-6).

20-5. Playing Next Stroke from Where Previous Stroke Played

When, under the Rules, a player elects or is required to play his next stroke from where a previous stroke was played, he shall proceed as follows: if the stroke is to be played from the teeing ground, the ball to be played shall be played from anywhere within the teeing ground and may be teed; if the stroke is to be played from through the green or a hazard, it shall be dropped; if the stroke is to be played on the putting green, it shall be placed.

PENALTY FOR BREACH OF RULE 20-5: *Match play – Loss of hole; Stroke play – Two strokes.*

20-6. Lifting Ball Incorrectly Substituted, Dropped or Placed

A ball incorrectly substituted, dropped or placed in a wrong place or otherwise not in accordance with the Rules but not played may be lifted, without penalty, and the player shall then proceed correctly.

20-7. Playing from Wrong Place

For a ball played from outside the teeing ground or from a wrong teeing ground – see Rule 11-4 and -5.

a. Match Play

If a player plays a stroke with a ball which has been dropped or placed in a wrong place, *he shall lose the hole.*

b. Stroke Play

If a competitor plays a stroke with his ball in play (i) which has been dropped or placed in a wrong place or (ii) which has been moved and not replaced in a case where the Rules require replacement, *he shall,* provided a serious breach has not occurred, *incur the penalty prescribed by the applicable Rule* and play out the hole with the ball.

If, after playing from a wrong place, a competitor becomes aware of that fact and believes that a serious breach may be involved, he may, provided he has not played a stroke from the next teeing ground or, in the case of the last hole of the round, left the putting green, declare that he will play out the hole with a second ball dropped or placed in accordance with the Rules. The competitor shall report the facts to the Committee before returning his score card; if he fails to do so, *he shall be disqualified.* The Committee shall determine whether a serious breach of the Rule occurred. If so, the score with the second ball shall count and *the competitor shall add two penalty strokes to his score with that ball.*

If a serious breach has occurred and the competitor has failed to correct it as prescribed above, *he shall be disqualified.*

Note: If a competitor plays a second ball, penalty strokes incurred by playing the ball ruled not to count and strokes subsequently taken with that ball shall be disregarded.

RULE 21. CLEANING BALL

A ball on the putting green may be cleaned when lifted under Rule 16-1b. Elsewhere, a ball may be cleaned when lifted except when it has been lifted:

a. To determine if it is unfit for play (Rule 5-3);

b. For identification (Rule 12-2), in which case it may be cleaned only to the extent necessary for identification; or

c. Because it is interfering with or assisting play (Rule 22).

If a player cleans his ball during play of a hole except as provided in this Rule, *he shall incur a penalty of one stroke* and the ball, if lifted, shall be replaced.

If a player who is required to replace a ball fails to do so, *he shall incur the penalty* for breach of Rule 20-3a, but no additional penalty under Rule 21 shall be applied.

Exception: If a player incurs a penalty for failing to act in accordance with Rule 5-3, 12-2 or 22, no additional penalty under Rule 21 shall be applied.

RULE 22. BALL INTERFERING WITH OR ASSISTING PLAY

Any player may:

a. Lift his ball if he considers that the ball might assist any other player or

b. Have any other ball lifted if he considers that the ball might interfere with his play or assist the play of any other player, but this may not be done while another ball is in motion. In stroke play, a player required to lift his ball may play first rather than lift. A ball lifted under this Rule shall be replaced.

PENALTY FOR BREACH OF RULE:
Match play – Loss of hole; Stroke play – Two strokes.

Note: Except on the putting green, the ball may not be cleaned when lifted under this Rule – see Rule 21.

RULE 23. LOOSE IMPEDIMENTS

Definition

"Loose impediments" are natural objects such as stones, leaves, twigs, branches and the like, dung, worms and insects and casts or heaps made by them, provided they are not fixed or growing, are not solidly embedded and do not adhere to the ball.

Sand and loose soil are loose impediments on the <u>putting green</u> but not elsewhere.

Snow and natural ice, other than frost, are either <u>casual water</u> or loose impediments, at the option of the player. Manufactured ice is an <u>obstruction</u>.

Dew and frost are not loose impediments.

23-1. Relief

Except when both the <u>loose impediment</u> and the ball lie in or touch the same <u>hazard</u>, any loose impediment may be removed without penalty. If the ball moves, see Rule 18-2c.

When a ball is in motion, a loose impediment which might influence the movement of the ball shall not be removed.

PENALTY FOR BREACH OF RULE:
Match play – Loss of hole; Stroke play – Two strokes.

(Searching for ball in hazard – see Rule 12-1.)

(Touching line of putt – see Rule 16-1a.)

RULE 24. OBSTRUCTIONS

Definition

An "obstruction" is anything artificial, including the artificial surfaces and sides of roads and paths and manufactured ice, except:

a. Objects defining <u>out of bounds</u>, such as walls, fences, stakes and railings;

b. Any part of an immovable artificial object which is out of bounds; and

c. Any construction declared by the Committee to be an integral part of the course.

24-1. Movable Obstruction

A player may obtain relief from a movable <u>obstruction</u> as follows:

a. If the ball does not lie in or on the obstruction, the obstruction may be removed. If the ball moves, it shall be replaced, and there is no penalty provided that the movement of the ball is directly attributable to the removal of the obstruction. Otherwise, Rule 18-2a applies.

b. If the ball lies in or on the obstruction, the ball may be lifted, without penalty, and the obstruction removed. The ball shall <u>through the green</u> or in a <u>hazard</u> be dropped, or on the <u>putting green</u> be placed, as near as possible to the spot directly under the place where the ball lay in or on the obstruction, but not nearer the hole.

The ball may be cleaned when lifted under Rule 24-1.

When a ball is in motion, an obstruction which might influence the movement of the ball, other than an attended flagstick or equipment of the players, shall not be removed.

Note: If a ball to be dropped or placed under this Rule is not immediately recoverable, another ball may be substituted.

24-2. Immovable Obstruction
a. Interference

Interference by an immovable <u>obstruction</u> occurs when a ball lies in or on the obstruction, or so close to the obstruction that the obstruction interferes with the player's <u>stance</u> or the area of his intended swing. If the player's ball lies on the <u>putting green</u>, interference also occurs if an immovable obstruction on the putting green intervenes on his line of putt. Otherwise, intervention on the line of play is not, of itself, interference under this Rule.

b. Relief

Except when the ball is in a <u>water hazard</u> or a <u>lateral water hazard</u>, a player may obtain relief from interference by an immovable <u>obstruction</u>, without penalty, as follows:

(i) **Through the Green:** If the ball lies <u>through the green</u>, the point on the <u>course</u> nearest to where the ball lies shall be determined (without crossing over, through or under the obstruction) which (a) is not nearer the hole, (b) avoids interference (as defined) and (c) is not in a <u>hazard</u> or on a <u>putting green</u>. The player shall lift the ball and drop it within one club-length of the point thus determined on a part of the course which fulfils (a), (b) and (c) above.

Note: The prohibition against crossing over, through or under the <u>obstruction</u> does not apply to the artificial surfaces and sides of roads and paths or when the ball lies in or on the obstruction.

(ii) **In a Bunker:** If the ball is in a <u>bunker</u>, the player shall lift and drop the ball in accordance with Clause (i) above,

except that the ball must be dropped in the bunker.

(iii) **On the Putting Green:** If the ball lies on the <u>putting green</u>, the player shall lift the ball and place it in the nearest position to where it lay which affords relief from interference, but not nearer the hole nor in a hazard.

The ball may be cleaned when lifted under Rule 24-2b.

(Ball rolling to a position where there is interference by the condition from which relief was taken – see Rule 20-2c(v).)

Exception: A player may not obtain relief under Rule 24-2b if (a) it is clearly unreasonable for him to play a stroke because of interference by anything other than an immovable obstruction or (b) interference by an immovable obstruction would occur only through use of an unnecessarily abnormal stance, swing or direction of play.

Note 1: If a ball is in a <u>water hazard</u> (including a <u>lateral water hazard</u>), the player is not entitled to relief without penalty from interference by an immovable obstruction. The player shall play the ball as it lies or proceed under Rule 26-1.

Note 2: If a ball to be dropped or placed under this Rule is not immediately recoverable, another ball may be substituted.

c. Ball Lost

Except in a <u>water hazard</u> or a <u>lateral water hazard</u>, if there is reasonable evidence that a ball is lost in an immovable obstruction, the player may, without penalty, substitute another ball and follow the procedure prescribed in Rule 24-2b. For the purpose of applying this Rule, the ball shall be deemed to lie at the spot where it entered the obstruction. If the ball is lost in an underground drain pipe or culvert the entrance to which is in a <u>hazard</u>, a ball must be dropped in that hazard or the player may proceed under Rule 26-1, if applicable.

PENALTY FOR BREACH OF RULE:
Match play – Loss of hole; Stroke play – Two strokes.

RULE 25. ABNORMAL GROUND CONDITIONS AND WRONG PUTTING GREEN

Definitions

"Casual water" is any temporary accumulation of water on the <u>course</u> which is visible before or after the player takes his <u>stance</u> and is not in a <u>water hazard</u>. Snow and natural ice, other than frost, are either casual water or <u>loose impediments</u>, at the option of the player. Manufactured ice is an <u>obstruction</u>. Dew and frost are not casual water. A ball is in casual water when it lies in or any part of it touches the casual water.

"Ground under repair" is any portion of the <u>course</u> so marked by order of the Committee or so declared by its authorised representative. It includes material piled for removal and a hole made by a greenkeeper, even if not so marked. Stakes and lines defining ground under repair are in such ground. Stakes defining ground under repair are obstructions. The margin of ground under repair extends vertically downwards, but not upwards. A ball is in ground under repair when it lies in or any part of it touches the ground under repair.

Note 1: Grass cuttings and other material left on the course which have been abandoned and are not intended to be

removed are not ground under repair unless so marked.

Note 2: The Committee may make a Local Rule prohibiting play from ground under repair or an environmentally-sensitive area which has been defined as ground under repair.

25-1. Casual Water, Ground Under Repair and Certain Damage to Course
a. Interference

Interference by <u>casual water</u>, <u>ground under repair</u> or a hole, cast or runway made by a burrowing animal, a reptile or a bird occurs when a ball lies in or touches any of these conditions or when such a condition on the <u>course</u> interferes with the player's <u>stance</u> or the area of his intended swing.

If the player's ball lies on the <u>putting green</u>, interference also occurs if such condition on the putting green intervenes on his line of putt.

If interference exists, the player may either play the ball as it lies (unless prohibited by Local Rule) or take relief as provided in Clause b.

Note: The Committee may make a Local Rule denying the player relief from interference with his stance by all or any of the conditions covered by this Rule.

b. Relief

If the player elects to take relief, he shall proceed as follows:

(i) **Through the Green:** If the ball lies <u>through the green</u>, the point on the <u>course</u> nearest to where the ball lies shall be determined which (a) is not nearer the hole, (b) avoids interference by the condition, and (c) is not in a <u>hazard</u> or on a <u>putting green</u>. The player shall lift the ball and drop it without penalty within one club-length of the point thus determined on a part of the course which fulfils (a), (b) and (c) above.

(ii) **In a Hazard:** If the ball is in a <u>hazard</u>, the player shall lift and drop the ball either:

(a) Without penalty, in the hazard, as near as possible to the spot where the ball lay, but not nearer the hole, on a part of the course which affords maximum available relief from the condition; or

(b) *Under penalty of one stroke*, outside the hazard, keeping the point where the ball lay directly between the hole and the spot on which the ball is dropped, with no limit to how far behind the hazard the ball may be dropped.

Exception: If a ball is in a <u>water hazard</u> (including a <u>lateral water hazard</u>), the player is not entitled to relief without penalty from a hole, cast or runway made by a burrowing animal, a reptile or a bird. The player shall play the ball as it lies or proceed under Rule 26-1.

(iii) **On the Putting Green:** If the ball lies on the <u>putting green</u>, the player shall lift the ball and place it without penalty in the nearest position to where it lay which affords maximum available relief from the condition, but not nearer the hole nor in a <u>hazard</u>.

The ball may be cleaned when lifted under Rule 25-1b. (Ball rolling to a position where there is interference by the condition from which relief was taken – see Rule 20-2c(v).)

Exception: A player may not obtain relief under Rule 25-1b if (a) it is clearly unreasonable for him to play a stroke because of interference by anything other than a con-

dition covered by Rule 25-1a or (b) interference by such a condition would occur only through use of an unnecessarily abnormal stance, swing or direction of play.

Note: If a ball to be dropped or placed under this Rule is not immediately recoverable, another ball may be substituted.

c. Ball Lost Under Condition Covered by Rule 25-1

It is a question of fact whether a ball lost after having been struck towards a condition covered by Rule 25-1 is lost under such condition. In order to treat the ball as lost under such condition, there must be reasonable evidence to that effect. In the absence of such evidence, the ball must be treated as a lost ball and Rule 27 applies.

(i)   **Outside a Hazard:** If a ball is lost outside a <u>hazard</u> under a condition covered by Rule 25-1, the player may take relief as follows: the point on the <u>course</u> nearest to where the ball last crossed the margin of the area shall be determined which (a) is not nearer the hole than where the ball last crossed the margin, (b) avoids interference by the condition and (c) is not in a hazard or on a <u>putting green</u>. He shall drop a ball without penalty within one club-length of the point thus determined on a part of the course which fulfils (a), (b) and (c) above.

(ii)   **In a Hazard:** If a ball is lost in a <u>hazard</u> under a condition covered by Rule 25-1, the player may drop a ball either:

(a) Without penalty, in the hazard, as near as possible to the point at which the original ball last crossed the margin of the area, but not nearer the hole, on a part of the course which affords maximum available relief from the condition;

or

(b) *Under penalty of one stroke,* outside the hazard, keeping the point at which the original ball last crossed the margin of the hazard directly between the hole and the spot on which the ball is dropped, with no limit to how far behind the hazard the ball may be dropped.

Exception: If a ball is in a <u>water hazard</u> (including a <u>lateral water hazard</u>), the player is not entitled to relief without penalty for a ball lost in a hole, cast or runway made by a burrowing animal, a reptile or a bird. The player shall proceed under Rule 26-1.

25-2. Embedded Ball

A ball embedded in its own pitch-mark in the ground in any closely-mown area <u>through the green</u> may be lifted, cleaned and dropped, without penalty, as near as possible to the spot where it lay but not nearer the hole. The ball when dropped must first strike a part of the course through the green. "Closely-mown area" means any area of the <u>course</u>, including paths through the rough, cut to fairway height or less.

25-3. Wrong Putting Green

A player must not play a ball which lies on a <u>putting green</u> other than that of the hole being played. The ball must be lifted and the player must proceed as follows: The point on the course nearest to where the ball lies shall be determined which (a) is not nearer the hole and (b) is not in a <u>hazard</u> or on a putting green. The player shall lift the ball and drop it without penalty within one club-length of the point thus determined on a part of the course which fulfils (a) and (b) above. The ball may be cleaned when so lifted.

Note: Unless otherwise prescribed by the Committee, the term "a putting green

other than that of the hole being played" includes a practice putting green or pitching green on the course.

PENALTY FOR BREACH OF RULE:

Match play – Loss of hole; Stroke play – Two strokes.

RULE 26. WATER HAZARDS

(Including Lateral Water Hazards)

Definitions

A "water hazard" is any sea, lake, pond, river, ditch, surface drainage ditch or other open water course (whether or not containing water) and anything of a similar nature.

All ground or water within the margin of a water hazard is part of the water hazard. The margin of a water hazard extends vertically upwards and downwards. Stakes and lines defining the margins of water hazards are in the hazards. Such stakes are obstructions. A ball is in a water hazard when it lies in or any part of it touches the water hazard.

Note 1: Water hazards (other than <u>lateral water hazards</u>) should be defined by yellow stakes or lines.

Note 2: The Committee may make a Local Rule prohibiting play from an environmentally-sensitive area which has been defined as a water hazard.

A "lateral water hazard" is a <u>water hazard</u> or that part of a water hazard so situated that it is not possible or is deemed by the Committee to be impracticable to drop a ball behind the water hazard in accordance with Rule 26-1b.

That part of a water hazard to be played as a lateral water hazard should be distinctively marked. A ball is in a lateral water hazard when it lies in or any part of it touches the lateral water hazard.

Note 1: Lateral water hazards should be defined by red stakes or lines.

Note 2: The Committee may make a Local Rule prohibiting play from an environmentally-sensitive area which has been defined as a lateral water hazard.

26-1. Ball in Water Hazard

It is a question of fact whether a ball lost after having been struck toward a <u>water hazard</u> is lost inside or outside the hazard. In order to treat the ball as lost in the hazard, there must be reasonable evidence that the ball lodged in it. In the absence of such evidence, the ball must be treated as a lost ball and Rule 27 applies.

If a ball is in or is lost in a water hazard (whether the ball lies in water or not), the player may *under penalty of one stroke:*

a. Play a ball as nearly as possible at the spot from which the original ball was last played (see Rule 20-5);

or

b. Drop a ball behind the water hazard, keeping the point at which the original ball last crossed the margin of the water hazard directly between the hole and the spot on which the ball is dropped, with no limit to how far behind the water hazard the ball may be dropped;

or

c. *As additional options available only if the ball last crossed the margin of a lateral water hazard,* drop a ball outside the water hazard within two club-lengths of and not nearer the hole than (i) the point where the original ball last crossed the margin of the water hazard or (ii) a point on the opposite margin of the water hazard equidistant from the hole.

The ball may be cleaned when lifted under this Rule.

(Ball moving in water in a water hazard – see Rule 14-6.)

26-2. Ball Played Within Water Hazard

a. Ball Comes to Rest in the Hazard

If a ball played from within a water hazard comes to rest in the same hazard after the stroke, the player may:

(i) proceed under Rule 26-1; or

(ii) *under penalty of one stroke,* play a ball as nearly as possible at the spot from which the last stroke from outside the hazard was played (see Rule 20-5).

If the player proceeds under Rule 26-1a, he may elect not to play the dropped ball. If he so elects, he may:

(a) proceed under Rule 26-1b, *adding the additional penalty of one stroke* prescribed by that Rule; or

(b) proceed under Rule 26-1c, if applicable, *adding the additional penalty of one stroke* prescribed by that Rule; or

(c) *add an additional penalty of one stroke* and play a ball as nearly as possible at the spot from which the last stroke from outside the hazard was played (see Rule 20-5).

b. Ball Lost or Unplayable Outside Hazard or Out of Bounds

If a ball played from within a water hazard is lost or declared unplayable outside the hazard or is out of bounds, the player, after taking *a penalty of one stroke* under Rule 27-1 or 28a, may:

(i) play a ball as nearly as possible at the spot in the hazard from which the original ball was last played (see Rule 20-5); or

(ii) proceed under Rule 26-1b, or if applicable Rule 26-1c, *adding the additional penalty of one stroke* prescribed by the Rule and using as the reference point the point where the original ball last crossed the margin of the hazard before it came to rest in the hazard; or

(iii) *add an additional penalty of one stroke* and play a ball as nearly as possible at the spot from which the last stroke from outside the hazard was played (see Rule 20-5).

Note 1: When proceeding under Rule 26-2b, the player is not required to drop a ball under Rule 27-1 or 28a. If he does drop a ball, he is not required to play it. He may alternatively proceed under Clause (ii) or (iii).

Note 2: If a ball played from within a water hazard is declared unplayable outside the hazard, nothing in Rule 26-2b precludes the player from proceeding under Rule 28b or c.

PENALTY FOR BREACH OF RULE:

Match play – Loss of hole; Stroke play – Two strokes.

RULE 27. BALL LOST OR OUT OF BOUNDS; PROVISIONAL BALL

If the original ball is lost in an immovable obstruction (Rule 24-2) or under a condition covered by Rule 25-1 (casual water, ground under repair and certain damage to the course), the player may proceed under the applicable Rule. If the original ball is lost in a water hazard, the player shall proceed under Rule 26.

Such Rules may not be used unless there is reasonable evidence that the ball is lost in an immovable obstruction, under a condition covered by Rule 25-1 or in a water hazard.

Definitions

A ball is "lost" if:

a. It is not found or identified as his by the player within five minutes after the player's side or his or their caddies have begun to search for it; or

b. The player has put another ball into play under the Rules, even though he may not have searched for the original ball; or

c. The player has played any stroke with a <u>provisional ball</u> from the place where the original ball is likely to be or from a point nearer the hole than that place, whereupon the provisional ball becomes the <u>ball in play</u>.

Time spent in playing a <u>wrong ball</u> is not counted in the five-minute period allowed for search.

"Out of bounds" is ground on which play is prohibited.

When out of bounds is defined by reference to stakes or a fence, or as being beyond stakes or a fence, the out of bounds line is determined by the nearest inside points of the stakes or fence posts at ground level excluding angled supports.

When out of bounds is defined by a line on the ground, the line itself is out of bounds.

The out of bounds line extends vertically upwards and downwards.

A ball is out of bounds when all of it lies out of bounds.

A player may stand out of bounds to play a ball lying within bounds.

A "provisional ball" is a ball played under Rule 27-2 for a ball which may be <u>lost</u> outside a <u>water hazard</u> or may be <u>out of bounds</u>.

27-1. Ball Lost or Out of Bounds

If a ball is <u>lost</u> outside a <u>water hazard</u> or is <u>out of bounds</u>, the player shall play a ball, *under penalty of one stroke,* as nearly as possible at the spot from which the original ball was last played (see Rule 20-5).

PENALTY FOR BREACH OF RULE 27-1:

Match play – Loss of hole; Stroke play – Two strokes.

27-2. Provisional Ball

a. Procedure

If a ball may be <u>lost</u> outside a <u>water hazard</u> or may be <u>out of bounds</u>, to save time the player may play another ball provisionally as nearly as possible at the spot from which the original ball was played (see Rule 20-5). The player shall inform his opponent in match play or his marker or a fellow-competitor in stroke play that he intends to play a <u>provisional ball</u>, and he shall play it before he or his partner goes forward to search for the original ball. If he fails to do so and plays another ball, such ball is not a provisional ball and becomes the <u>ball in play</u> *under penalty of stroke and distance* (Rule 27-1); the original ball is deemed to be lost.

b. When Provisional Ball Becomes Ball in Play

The player may play a provisional ball until he reaches the place where the original ball is likely to be. If he plays a stroke with the provisional ball from the place where the original ball is likely to be or from a point nearer the hole than that place, the original ball is deemed to be <u>lost</u> and the provisional ball becomes the ball in play under *penalty of stroke and distance* (Rule 27-1).

If the original ball is lost outside a water hazard or is out of bounds, the provisional ball becomes the ball in play, *under penalty of stroke and distance* (Rule 27-1).

c. When Provisional Ball to Be Abandoned

If the original ball is neither lost outside a water hazard nor out of bounds, the player shall abandon the provisional ball and continue play with the original ball. If he fails to do so, any further strokes played with the provisional ball shall constitute playing a wrong ball and the provisions of Rule 15 shall apply.

Note: If the original ball is in a water hazard, the player shall play the ball as it lies or proceed under Rule 26. If it is lost in a water hazard or unplayable, the player shall proceed under Rule 26 or 28, whichever is applicable.

RULE 28. BALL UNPLAYABLE

The player may declare his ball unplayable at any place on the course except when the ball is in a water hazard. The player is the sole judge as to whether his ball is unplayable.

If the player deems his ball to be unplayable, he shall, *under penalty of one stroke:*
a. Play a ball as nearly as possible at the spot from which the original ball was last played (see Rule 20-5);

or

b. Drop a ball within two club-lengths of the spot where the ball lay, but not nearer the hole;

or

c. Drop a ball behind the point where the ball lay, keeping that point directly between the hole and the spot on which the ball is dropped, with no limit to how far behind that point the ball may be dropped.

If the unplayable ball is in a bunker, the player may proceed under Clause a, b or c. If he elects to proceed under Clause b or c, a ball must be dropped in the bunker.

The ball may be cleaned when lifted under this Rule.

PENALTY FOR BREACH OF RULE:
Match play – Loss of hole; Stroke play – Two strokes.

OTHER FORMS OF PLAY

RULE 29. THREESOMES AND FOURSOMES
Definitions

Threesome: A match in which one plays against two, and each side plays one ball.

Foursome: A match in which two play against two, and each side plays one ball.

29-1. General

In a threesome or a foursome, during any stipulated round the partners shall play alternately from the teeing grounds and alternately during the play of each hole. Penalty strokes do not affect the order of play.

29-2. Match Play

If a player plays when his partner should have played, *his side shall lose the hole.*

29-3. Stroke Play

If the partners play a stroke or strokes in incorrect order, such stroke or strokes shall be cancelled and *the side shall incur a penalty of two strokes.* The side shall correct the error by playing a ball in correct order as nearly as possible at the spot from which it first played in incorrect order (see Rule 20-5). If the side plays a stroke from the next teeing ground without first correcting the error or, in the case of the last hole of the round, leaves the putting green without declaring its intention to correct the error, *the side shall be disqualified.*

RULE 30. THREE-BALL, BEST-BALL AND FOUR-BALL MATCH PLAY
Definitions

Three-Ball: A match play competition in which three play against one another, each playing his own ball. Each player is playing two distinct matches.

Best-Ball: A match in which one plays against the better ball of two or the best ball of three players.

Four-Ball: A match in which two play their better ball against the better ball of two other players.

30-1. Rules of Golf Apply

The Rules of Golf, so far as they are not at variance with the following special Rules, shall apply to three-ball, best-ball and four-ball matches.

30-2. Three-Ball Match Play
a. Ball at Rest Moved by an Opponent

Except as otherwise provided in the Rules, if the player's ball is touched or moved by an opponent, his caddie or equipment other than during search, Rule 18-3b applies. *That opponent shall incur a penalty stroke in his match with the player,* but not in his match with the other opponent.

b. Ball Deflected or Stopped by an Opponent Accidentally

If a player's ball is accidentally deflected or stopped by an opponent, his caddie or equipment, no penalty shall be incurred. In his match with that opponent the player may play the ball as it lies or, before another stroke is played by either side, he may cancel the stroke and play a ball without penalty as nearly as possible at the spot from which the original ball was last played (see Rule 20-5). In his match with the other opponent, the ball shall be played as it lies.

Exception: Ball striking person attending flagstick – see Rule 17-3b.

(Ball purposely deflected or stopped by opponent – see Rule 1-2.)

30-3. Best-Ball and Four-Ball Match Play
a. Representation of Side

A side may be represented by one partner for all or any part of a match; all partners need not be present. An absent partner may join a match between holes, but not during play of a hole.

b. Maximum of Fourteen Clubs

The side shall be penalised for a breach of Rule 4-4 by any partner.

c. Order of Play

Balls belonging to the same side may be played in the order the side considers best.

d. Wrong Ball

If a player plays a stroke with a wrong ball except in a hazard, *he shall be disqualified for that hole,* but his partner incurs no penalty even if the wrong ball belongs to him. If the wrong ball belongs to another player, its owner shall place a ball on the spot from which the wrong ball was first played.

e. Disqualification of Side

(i) *A side shall be disqualified* for a breach of any of the following by any partner:

Rule 1-3 – Agreement to Waive Rules.
Rule 4-1, -2 or -3 – Clubs.
Rule 5-1 or -2 – The Ball.
Rule 6-2a – Handicap (playing off higher handicap).
Rule 6-4 – Caddie.
Rule 6-7 – Undue Delay; Slow Play (repeated offence).
Rule 14-3 – Artificial Devices and Unusual Equipment.

(ii) *A side shall be disqualified* for a breach of any of the following by all partners:

Rule 6-3 – Time of Starting and Groups.
Rule 6-8 – Discontinuance of Play.

f. Effect of Other Penalties

If a player's breach of a Rule assists his partner's play or adversely affects an opponent's play, *the partner incurs the applicable penalty in addition to any penalty incurred by the player.*

In all other cases where a player incurs a penalty for breach of a Rule, the penalty shall not apply to his partner. Where the penalty is stated to be loss of hole, the effect shall be to disqualify the player for that hole.

g. Another Form of Match Played Concurrently

In a best-ball or four-ball match when another form of match is played concurrently, the above special Rules shall apply.

RULE 31. FOUR-BALL STROKE PLAY

In four-ball stroke play two competitors play as partners, each playing his own ball. The lower score of the partners is the score for the hole. If one partner fails to complete the play of a hole, there is no penalty.

31-1. Rules of Golf Apply

The Rules of Golf, so far as they are not at variance with the following special Rules, shall apply to four-ball stroke play.

31-2. Representation of Side

A side may be represented by either partner for all or any part of a stipulated round; both partners need not be present. An absent competitor may join his partner between holes, but not during play of a hole.

31-3. Maximum of Fourteen Clubs

The side shall be penalised for a breach of Rule 4-4 by either partner.

31-4. Scoring

The marker is required to record for each hole only the gross score of whichever partner's score is to count. The gross scores to count must be individually identifiable; otherwise *the side shall be disqualified.* Only one of the partners need be responsible for complying with Rule 6-6b.

(Wrong score – see Rule 31-7a.)

31-5. Order of Play

Balls belonging to the same side may be played in the order the side considers best.

31-6. Wrong Ball

If a competitor plays a stroke or strokes with a wrong ball except in a hazard, *he shall add two penalty strokes to his score for the hole* and shall then play the correct ball. His partner incurs no penalty even if the wrong ball belongs to him.

If the wrong ball belongs to another competitor, its owner shall place a ball on the spot from which the wrong ball was first played.

31-7. Disqualification Penalties
a. Breach by One Partner

A side shall be disqualified from the competition for a breach of any of the following by either partner:

Rule 1-3 – Agreement to Waive Rules.
Rule 3-4 – Refusal to Comply with Rule.
Rule 4-1, -2 or -3 –Clubs.
Rule 5-1 or -2 –The Ball.
Rule 6-2b – Handicap (playing off higher handicap; failure to record handicap).
Rule 6-4 – Caddie.
Rule 6-6b – Signing and Returning Card.
Rule 6-6d – Wrong Score for Hole, i.e. when the recorded score of the partner whose score is to count is lower than actually taken. If the recorded score of the partner whose score is to count is higher than actually taken, it must stand as returned.

Rule 6-7 – Undue Delay; Slow Play (repeated offence).
Rule 7-1 – Practice Before or Between Rounds.
Rule 14-3 – Artificial Devices and Unusual Equipment.
Rule 31-4 – Gross Scores to Count Not Individually Identifiable.

b. Breach by Both Partners

A side shall be disqualified:

(i) for a breach by both partners of Rule 6-3 (Time of Starting and Groups) or Rule 6-8 (Discontinuance of Play), or

(ii) if, at the same hole, each partner is in breach of a Rule the penalty for which is disqualification from the competition or for a hole.

c. For the Hole Only

In all other cases where a breach of a Rule would entail disqualification, *the competitor shall be disqualified only for the hole at which the breach occurred.*

31-8. Effect of Other Penalties

If a competitor's breach of a Rule assists his partner's play, *the partner incurs the applicable penalty in addition to any penalty incurred by the competitor.*

In all other cases where a competitor incurs a penalty for breach of a Rule, the penalty shall not apply to his partner.

RULE 32. BOGEY, PAR AND STABLEFORD COMPETITONS
32-1. Conditions

Bogey, par and Stableford competitions are forms of stroke competition in which play is against a fixed score at each hole. The Rules for stroke play, so far as they are not at variance with the following special Rules, apply.

a. Bogey and Par Competitions

The reckoning for bogey and par competitions is made as in match play. Any hole for which a competitor makes no return shall be regarded as a loss. The winner is the competitor who is most successful in the aggregate of holes.

The marker is responsible for marking only the gross number of strokes for each hole where the competitor makes a net score equal to or less than the fixed score.

Note: Maximum of 14 Clubs – Penalties as in match play – see Rule 4-4.

b. Stableford Competitions

The reckoning in Stableford competitions is made by points awarded in relation to a fixed score at each hole as follows:

Hole Played in	Points
More than one over fixed score or no score returned	0
One over fixed score	1
Fixed score	2
One under fixed score	3
Two under fixed score	4
Three under fixed score	5
Four under fixed score	6

The winner is the competitor who scores the highest number of points.

The marker shall be responsible for marking only the gross number of strokes at each hole where the competitor's net score earns one or more points.

Note: Maximum of 14 Clubs (Rule 4-4) – Penalties applied as follows: From total points scored for the round, deduction of two points for each hole at which any

breach occurred; maximum deduction per round: four points.

32-2. Disqualification Penalties

a. From the Competition

A competitor shall be disqualified from the competition for a breach of any of the following

Rule 1-3 – Agreement to Waive Rules.

Rule 3-4 – Refusal to Comply with Rule.

Rule 4-1, -2 or -3 – Clubs.

Rule 5-1 or -2 – The Ball.

Rule 6-2b – Handicap (playing off higher handicap; failure to record handicap).

Rule 6-3 – Time of Starting and Groups.

Rule 6-4 – Caddie.

Rule 6-6b – Signing and Returning Card.

Rule 6-6d – Wrong Score for Hole, except that no penalty shall be incurred when a breach of this Rule does not affect the result of the hole.

Rule 6-7 – Undue Delay; Slow Play (repeated offence).

Rule 6-8 – Discontinuance of Play.

Rule 7-1 – Practice Before or Between Rounds.

Rule 14-3 – Artificial Devices and Unusual Equipment.

b. For a Hole

In all other cases where a breach of a Rule would entail disqualification, *the competitor shall be disqualified only for the hole at which the breach occurred.*

ADMINISTRATION

RULE 33. THE COMMITTEE

33-1. Conditions; Waiving Rule

The Committee shall lay down the conditions under which a competition is to be played.

The Committee has no power to waive a Rule of Golf.

Certain special rules governing stroke play are so substantially different from those governing match play that combining the two forms of play is not practicable and is not permitted. The results of matches played and the scores returned in these circumstances shall not be accepted.

In stroke play the Committee may limit a referee's duties.

33-2. The Course

a. Defining Bounds and Margins

The Committee shall define accurately:

(i)   the course and out of bounds,

(ii)   the margins of water hazards and lateral water hazards,

(iii)   ground under repair, and

(iv)   obstructions and integral parts of the course.

b. New Holes

New holes should be made on the day on which a stroke competition begins and at such other times as the Committee considers necessary, provided all competitors in a single round play with each hole cut in the same position.

Exception: When it is impossible for a damaged hole to be repaired so that it conforms with the Definition, the Committee may make a new hole in a nearby similar position.

Note: Where a single round is to be played on more than one day, the Committee may provide in the conditions of a competition that the holes and teeing grounds may be differently situated on each day of the competition, provided that, on any one day, all competitors play with each hole and each teeing ground in the same position.

c. Practice Ground

Where there is no practice ground available outside the area of a competition course, the Committee should lay down the area on which players may practise on any day of a competition, if it is practicable to do so. On any day of a stroke competition, the Committee should not normally permit practice on or to a putting green or from a hazard of the competition course.

d. Course Unplayable

If the Committee or its authorised representative considers that for any reason the course is not in a playable condition or that there are circumstances which render the proper playing of the game impossible, it may, in match play or stroke play, order a temporary suspension of play or, in stroke play, declare play null and void and cancel all scores for the round in question. When play has been temporarily suspended, it shall be resumed from where it was discontinued, even though resumption occurs on a subsequent day. When a round is cancelled, all penalties incurred in that round are cancelled. (Procedure in discontinuing play – see Rule 6-8.)

33-3. Times of Starting and Groups

The Committee shall lay down the times of starting and, in stroke play, arrange the groups in which competitors shall play.

When a match play competition is played over an extended period, the Committee shall lay down the limit of time within which each round shall be completed. When players are allowed to arrange the date of their match within these limits, the Committee should announce that the match must be played at a stated time on the last day of the period unless the players agree to a prior date.

33-4. Handicap Stroke Table

The Committee shall publish a table indicating the order of holes at which handicap strokes are to be given or received.

33-5. Score Card

In stroke play, the Committee shall issue for each competitor a score card containing the date and the competitor's name or, in foursome or four-ball stroke play, the competitors' names.

In stroke play, the Committee is responsible for the addition of scores and application of the handicap recorded on the card.

In four-ball stroke play, the Committee is responsible for recording the better-ball score for each hole and in the process applying the handicaps recorded on the card, and adding the better-ball scores.

In bogey, par and Stableford competitions, the Committee is responsible for applying the handicap recorded on the card and determining the result of each hole and the overall result or points total.

33-6. Decision of Ties

The Committee shall announce the manner, day and time for the decision of a halved match or of a tie, whether played on level terms or under handicap.

A halved match shall not be decided by stroke play. A tie in stroke play shall not be decided by a match.

33-7. Disqualification Penalty; Committee Discretion

A penalty of disqualification may in exceptional individual cases be waived, modified or imposed if the Committee considers such action warranted.

Any penalty less than disqualification shall not be waived or modified.

33-8. Local Rules

a. Policy

The Committee may make and publish Local Rules for abnormal conditions if they are consistent with the policy of the Governing Authority for the country concerned as set forth in Appendix I to these Rules.

b. Waiving Penalty

A penalty imposed by a Rule of Golf shall not be waived by a Local Rule.

RULE 34. DISPUTES AND DECISIONS

34-1. Claims and Penalties

a. Match Play

In match play if a claim is lodged with the Committee under Rule 2-5, a decision should be given as soon as possible so that the state of the match may, if necessary, be adjusted.

If a claim is not made within the time limit provided by Rule 2-5, it shall not be considered unless it is based on facts previously unknown to the player making the claim and the player making the claim had been given wrong information (Rules 6-2a and 9) by an opponent. In any case, no later claim shall be considered after the result of the match has been officially announced, unless the Committee is satisfied that the opponent knew he was giving wrong information.

There is no time limit on applying the disqualification penalty for a breach of Rule 1-3.

b. Stroke Play

Except as provided below, in stroke play, no penalty shall be rescinded, modified or imposed after the competition has closed. A competition is deemed to have closed when the result has been officially announced or, in stroke play qualifying followed by match play, when the player has teed off in the first match.

Exceptions: A penalty of disqualification shall be imposed after the competition has closed if a competitor:

(i) was in breach of Rule 1-3 (Agreement to Waive Rules); or

(ii)   returned a score card on which he had recorded a handicap which, before the competition closed, he knew was higher than that to which he was entitled, and this affected the number of strokes received (Rule 6-2b); or

(iii)   returned a score for any hole lower than actually taken (Rule 6-6d) for any reason other than failure to include a penalty which, before the competition closed, he did not know he had incurred; or

(iv)   knew, before the competition closed, that he had been in breach of any other Rule for which the prescribed penalty is disqualification.

34-2. Referee's Decision

If a referee has been appointed by the Committee, his decision shall be final.

34-3. Committee's Decision

In the absence of a referee, any dispute or doubtful point on the Rules shall be referred to the Committee, whose decision shall be final.

If the Committee cannot come to a decision, it shall refer the dispute or doubtful point to the Rules of Golf Committee of the Royal and Ancient Golf Club of St. Andrews, whose decision shall be final.

If the dispute or doubtful point has not been referred to the Rules of Golf Committee, the player or players have the right to refer an agreed statement through the Secretary of the Club to the Rules of Golf Committee for an opinion as to the correctness of the decision given. The reply will be sent to the Secretary of the Club or Clubs concerned.

If play is conducted other than in accordance with the Rules of Golf, the Rules of Golf Committee will not give a decision on any question.

APPENDIX I

LOCAL RULES (RULE 33-8) AND CONDITIONS OF THE COMPETITION (RULE 33-1)

PART A   LOCAL RULES

Rule 33-8 provides, "The Committee may make and publish Local Rules for abnormal conditions if they are consistent with the policy of the Governing Authority for the country concerned as set forth in Appendix I to these Rules. A penalty imposed by a Rule of Golf shall not be waived by a Local Rule."

Such abnormal conditions may include those listed below. Otherwise, detailed information regarding acceptable and prohibited Local Rules is provided in "Decisions on the Rules of Golf" under Rule 33-8.

If local conditions interfere with the proper playing of the game and it is considered necessary to modify a Rule of Golf, the approval of the Governing Authority must be obtained.

1. Obstructions

a. General

Clarifying the status of objects which may be obstructions (Rule 24).

Declaring any construction to be an integral part of the course and, accordingly, not an obstruction, e.g. built-up sides of teeing grounds, putting greens and bunkers (Rules 24 and 33-2a).

b. Stones in Bunkers

Allowing the removal of stones in bunkers by declaring them to be "movable obstructions" (Rule 24).

c. Roads and Paths

(i)   Declaring artificial surfaces and sides of roads and paths to be integral parts of the course, or

(ii)   Providing relief of the type afforded under Rule 24-2b from roads and paths not having artificial surfaces and sides if they could unfairly affect play.

d. Fixed Sprinkler Heads

Providing relief from intervention by fixed sprinkler heads within two club-lengths of the putting green when the ball lies within two club-lengths of the sprinkler head.

e. Protection of Young Trees

Providing relief for the protection of young trees.

f. Temporary Obstructions

Specimen Local Rules for temporary obstructions (e.g. grandstands, television cables and equipment, etc). for application in Tournament Play are available from the Royal and Ancient Golf Club of St. Andrews.

2. Areas of the Course Requiring Preservation

Assisting preservation of the course by defining areas, including turf nurseries, young plantations and other parts of the course under cultivation, as "ground under repair" from which play is prohibited.

3. Unusual Damage to the Course or

Accumulation of Leaves (or the like)
Declaring such areas to be "ground under repair" (Rule 25). The Committee may, by Local Rule, deny relief from interference with a player's stance by such areas – see Note to Rule 25-1a.
Note: For relief from aeration holes see Specimen Local Rule 8 in Part B of this Appendix.

4. Extreme Wetness, Mud, Poor Conditions and Protection of Course

a. Lifting an Embedded Ball, Cleaning
Where the ground is unusually soft, the Committee may, by temporary Local Rule, allow the lifting of a ball which is embedded in its own pitch-mark in the ground in an area "through the green" which is not "closely mown" (Rule 25-2) if it is satisfied that the proper playing of the game would otherwise be prevented. The Local Rule shall be for that day only or for a short period, and if practicable shall be confined to specified areas. The Committee shall withdraw the Local Rule as soon as conditions warrant and should not print it on the score card.

In similarly adverse conditions, the Committee may, by temporary Local Rule, permit the cleaning of a ball "through the green".

b. "Preferred Lies" and "Winter Rules"
Adverse conditions, including the poor condition of the course or the existence of mud, are sometimes so general, particularly during winter months, that the Committee may decide to grant relief by temporary Local Rule either to protect the course or to promote fair and pleasant play. Such Local Rule shall be withdrawn as soon as conditions warrant.

5. Environmentally-Sensitive Areas
When the Committee is required to prohibit play from environmentally-sensitive areas which are on or adjoin the course, it should make a Local Rule clarifying the relief procedure.

An environmentally-sensisitive area is an area so declared by an appropriate authority, entry into and/or play from which is prohibited for environmental reasons. Such an area may be defined as ground under repair, a water hazard, a lateral water hazard or out of bounds at the discretion of the Committee provided that, in the case of an environmentally-sensitive area which has been defined as a water hazard or a lateral water hazard, the area is, by Definition, a water hazard.
Note: The Committee may not declare an area to be environmentally-sensistive.

A specimen Local Rule is detailed in "Decisions on the Rules of Golf".

Other matters which the Committee could cover by Local Rule include:

6. Water Hazards

a. Lateral Water Hazards
Clarifying the status of sections of water hazards which may be lateral water hazards (Rule 26).

b. Provisional Ball
Permitting play of a provisional ball for a ball which may be in a water hazard of such character that it would be impracticable to determine whether the ball is in the hazard or to do so would unduly delay play. In such a case, if a provisional ball is played and the original ball is in a water hazard, the player may play the original ball as it lies or continue the provisional ball in play, but he may not proceed under Rule 26-1.

7. Defining Bounds and Margins
Specifying means used to define out of bounds, hazards, water hazards, lateral water hazards and ground under repair.

8. Dropping Zones
Establishing special areas in which balls may or shall be dropped when it is not feasible or practicable to proceed exactly in conformity with Rule 24-2b (Immovable Obstruction), Rule 25-1b or Rule 25-1c (Ground Under Repair), Rule 25-3 (Wrong Putting Green), Rule 26-1 (Water Hazards and Lateral Water Hazards) or Rule 28 (Ball Unplayable)

9. Priority on the Course
The Committee may make regulations governing Priority on the Course (see Etiquette).

PART B SPECIMEN LOCAL RULES

Within the policy set out in Part A of this Appendix, the Committee may adopt a Specimen Local Rule by referring, on a score card or notice board, to the examples given below. However, Specimen Local Rules 5, 6 or 7 should not be printed or referred to on a score card as they are all of limited duration.

1. Fixed Sprinkler Heads
All fixed sprinkler heads are immovable obstructions and relief from interference by them may be obtained under Rule 24-2. In addition, if such an obstruction on or within two club-lengths of the putting green of the hole being played intervenes on the line of play between the ball and the hole, the player may obtain relief, without penalty, as follows:

If the ball lies off the putting green but not in a hazard and is within two club-lengths of the intervening obstruction, it may be lifted, cleaned and dropped at the nearest point to where the ball lay which (a) is not nearer the hole, (b) avoids such intervention and (c) is not in a hazard or on a putting green.
PENALTY FOR BREACH OF LOCAL RULE: *Match play – Loss of Hole; Stroke play – Two strokes.*

2. Stones in Bunkers
Stones in bunkers are movable obstructions (Rule 24-1 applies)

3. Protection of Young Trees
Protection of young trees identified by __________________ . If such a tree interferes with a player's stance or the area of his intended swing, the ball must be lifted, without penalty, and dropped in accordance with the procedure prescribed in Rule 24-2b(i) (Immovable Obstruction). The ball may be cleaned when so lifted.
PENALTY FOR BREACH OF LOCAL RULE
Match play – Loss of hole; Stroke play – Two strokes.

4. Ground Under Repair: Play Prohibited
If a player's ball lies in an area of "ground under repair" from which play is prohibited, or if such an area of "ground under repair" interferes with the player's stance or the area of his intended swing the player must take relief under Rule 25-1.
PENALTY FOR BREACH OF LOCAL RULE
Match play – Loss of hole; Stroke play – Two strokes.

5. Lifting an Embedded Ball
(Specify the area if practicable) . . . through the green, a ball embedded in its own pitch-mark in ground other than sand may be lifted, cleaned and dropped, without penalty, as near as possible to the spot where it lay but not nearer the hole.
PENALTY FOR BREACH OF LOCAL RULE: *Match play – Loss of hole; Stroke play – Two strokes.*

6. Cleaning Ball
(Specify the area if practicable) . . . through the green a ball may be lifted, cleaned and replaced without penalty.
Note: The position of the ball shall be marked before it is lifted under this Local Rule – see Rule 20-1.

7. "Preferred Lies" and "Winter Rules"
A ball lying on any "closely mown area" through the green may, without penalty, be moved or may be lifted, cleaned and placed within six inches of where it originally lay, but not nearer the hole. After the ball has been so moved or placed, it is in play.
PENALTY FOR BREACH OF LOCAL RULE:
Match play – Loss of hole; Stroke play – Two strokes.

8. Aeration Holes
If a ball comes to rest in an aeration hole, the player may, without penalty, lift the ball and clean it. Through the green, the player shall drop the ball as near as possible to where it lay, but not nearer the hole. On the putting green, the player shall place the ball at the nearest spot not nearer the hole which avoids such situation.
PENALTY FOR BREACH OF LOCAL RULE: *Match play – Loss of hole; Stroke play – Two strokes.*

PART C CONDITIONS OF THE COMPETITION

Rule 33-1 provides, "The Committee shall lay down the conditions under which a competition is to be played". Such conditions should include many matters such as method of entry, eligibility, number of rounds to be played, settling ties, etc. which it is not appropriate to deal with in the Rules of Golf or this Appendix. Detailed information regarding such conditions is provided in "Decisions on the Rules of Golf" under Rule 33-1.

However, there are seven matters which might be covered in the Conditions of the Competition to which the Committee's attention is specifically drawn by way of a Note to the appropriate Rule. These are:

1. Specification of the Ball (Note to Rule 5-1)

a. List of Conforming Golf Balls
Arising from the regulations for ball-testing under Rule 5-1, a List of Conforming Golf Balls will be issued from time to time.

It is recommended that the List should be applied to all National and County (or equivalent) Championships and to all top-class events when restricted to low handicap players. In order to apply the List to a particular competition the Committee must lay this down in the Conditions of the Competition. This should be referred to in the Entry Form, and also a notice should be displayed on the Club notice board and at the 1st Tee along the following lines:

..............(Name of Event)..........................

...............(Date and Club)..........................

"The Ball (Note to Rule 5-1).
The ball the player uses shall be named on the current List of Conforming Golf Balls issued by the Royal and Ancient Golf Club of St. Andrews."

A penalty statement will be required and must be either:
(a) "PENALTY FOR BREACH OF CONDITION: *Disqualification.*"
or
(b) "PENALTY FOR BREACH OF CONDITION: *Match play – Loss of each hole at which a breach occurred. Stroke play – Two strokes for each hole at which a breach occurred.*"
If option (b) is adopted this only applies to use of a ball which, whilst not on the List of Conforming Golf Balls, does conform to the specifications set forth in Rule 5 and Appendix III. The penalty for use of a ball which does not so conform is disqualification.

b. One Ball Condition
If it is desired to prohibit changing brands and types of golf balls during a stipulated round, the following condition is recommended:

"Limitation on Balls Used During Round: (Note to Rule 5-1).
(i) "One Ball" Condition
During a stipulated round, the ball the player uses must be of the same brand and type as detailed by a single entry on the current List of Conforming Golf Balls.
PENALTY FOR BREACH OF CONDITION: *Match Play – At the conclusion of the hole at which the breach is discovered, the state of the match shall be adjusted by deducting one hole for each hole at which a breach occurred; maximum deduction per round: Two holes. Stroke Play – Two strokes for each hole at which any breach occurred; maximum penalty per round; Four strokes.*
(ii) Procedure When Breach Discovered
When a player discovers that he has used a ball in breach of this condition, he shall abandon that ball before playing from the next teeing ground and complete the round using a proper ball; otherwise, the player shall be disqualified. If discovery is made during play of a hole and the player elects to substitute a proper ball before completing that hole, the player shall place a proper ball on the spot where the ball used in breach of the condition lay."
Note: In Club events it is recommended that no such condition be applied.

2. Time of Starting (Note to Rule 6-3a)
If the Committee wishes to act in accordance with the Note, the following wording is recommended:

"If the player arrives at his starting point, ready to play, within five minutes after his starting time, in the absence of circumstances which warrant waiving the penalty of disqualification as provided in Rule 33-7, the penalty for failure to start on time is loss of the first hole to be played in match play or two strokes in stroke play. Penalty for lateness beyond five minutes is disqualification."

3. Pace of Play
The Committee may lay down pace of play guidelines, to help prevent slow play, in accordance with Note 2 to Rule 6-7.

4. Suspension of Play Due to a Dangerous Situation (Note to Rule 6-8b)
If the Committee wishes to act in accordance with the Note, the following wording is recommended:

"When play is suspended by the Committee for a dangerous situation (e.g. lightning, tornados, etc.) if the players in a match or group are between the play of two holes, they shall not resume play until the Committee has ordered a resumption of play. If they are in the process of playing a hole, they shall discontinue play immediately and shall not thereafter resume play until the Committee has ordered a resumption of play.

The signal for suspending play due to a dangerous situation will be
....
PENALTY FOR BREACH OF CONDITION: *Disqualification."*

5. Practice
The Committee may make regulations governing practice in accordance with the Note to Rule 7-1, Exception (c) to Rule 7-2, Note 2 to Rule 7 and Rule 33-2c.

6. Advice in Team Competitions
If the Committee wishes to act in accordance with the Note, the following wording is recommended:
"In accordance with the Note to Rule 8 of the Rules of Golf each team may appoint one person (in addition to the persons from whom advice may be asked under that Rule) who may give advice to members of that team. Such person *[if it is desired to insert any restriction on who may be nominated insert such restriction here]* shall be identified to the Committee before giving advice."

7. New Holes
The Committee may provide, in accordance with the Note to Rule 33-2b, that the holes and teeing grounds for a single round competition, being held on more than one day, may be differently situated on each day.

190

APPENDICES II AND III
Any design in a club or ball which is not covered by Rules 4 and 5 and Appendices II and III, or which might significantly change the nature of the game, will be ruled on by the Royal and Ancient Golf Club of St. Andrews and the United States Golf Association.

APPENDIX II
Design of Clubs
Clubs must not be substantially different from the traditional and customary form and make.
    Rule 4-1 prescribes general regulations for their design. The following paragraphs, which provide some specifications and clarify how Rule 4-1 is interpreted, should be read in conjunction with that Rule.
    Where a club, or part of a club, is required to have some specific property, this means that it must be designed and manufactured with the intention of having that property. The finished club or part must have that property within manufacturing tolerances appropriate to the material used.

4-1a. General
Adjustability – Exception for Putters. Clubs other than putters shall not be designed to be adjustable except for weight.
    Some other forms of adjustability are permitted in the design of a putter, provided that:
(i) the adjustment cannot be readily made;
(ii) all adjustable parts are firmly fixed and there is no reasonable likelihood of them working loose during a round; and
(iii) all configurations of adjustment conform with the Rules.
    The disqualification penalty for purposely changing the playing characteristics of a club during a stipulated round (Rule 4-2) applies to all clubs including a putter.
Note: It is recommended that all putters with adjustable parts be submitted to the Royal and

Ancient Golf Club of St. Andrews for a ruling.
4-1b. Shaft
Straightness. The shaft shall be straight from the top of the grip to a point not more than 5 inches (127 mm) above the sole, measured from the point where the shaft ceases to be straight along the axis of the bent part of the shaft and the neck and/or socket (See Fig. 1);

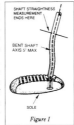

Figure I

Length. The overall length of the club shall be least 18 inches (457 mm) measured from the top of the grip along the axis of the shaft or a straight line extension of it to the sole of the club.
Alignment. When the club is in its normal address position the shaft shall be so aligned that:
(i) the projection of the straight part of the shaft on to the vertical plane through the toe and heel shall diverge from the vertical by at least ten degrees (See Fig. II);
(ii) the projection of the straight part of the shaft on to the vertical plane along the intended line of play shall not diverge from the vertical by more than 20 degrees (See Fig. III).

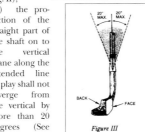

Figure II

Figure III

    Except for putters, all of the heel portion of the club shall lie within 0.625 inches (16 mm) of the plane containing the axis of the straight part of the shaft and the intended (horizontal) line of play (See Fig. IV).

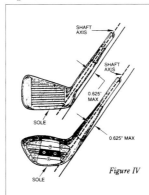

Figure IV

Bending and Twisting Properties. At any point along its length, the shaft shall:
(i) bend in such a way that the deflection is the same regardless of how the shaft is rotated about its longitudinal axis; and
(ii) twist the same amount in both directions.

Attachment to Clubhead. The shaft shall be attached to the clubhead at the heel either directly or through a neck and/or socket. The length from the top of the neck and/or socket to the sole of the club shall not exceed 5 inches (127 mm), measured along the axis of, and following any bend in, the neck and/or socket (See Fig. V).

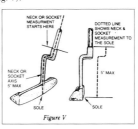

Figure V

Exception for Putters: The shaft or neck or socket of a putter may be fixed at any point in the head.
4-1c. Grip (See Fig. VI)
(i)   For clubs other than putters the grip must be circular in cross-section, except that a continuous, straight, slightly raised rib may be incorporated along the full length of the grip, and a slightly indented spiral is permitted on a wrapped grip or a replica of one.
(ii)   A putter grip may have a non-circular cross-section, provided the cross-section has no concavity, is symmetrical and remains generally similar throughout the length of the grip.
(iii)   The grip may be tapered but must not have any bulge or waist. Its cross-sectional dimension measured in any direction must not exceed 1.75 inches (45 mm).
(iv)   For clubs other than putters the axis of the grip must coincide with the axis of the shaft.
(v)   A putter may have more than one grip, provided each is circular in cross-section and the axis of each coincides with the axis of the shaft.

4-1d. Clubhead

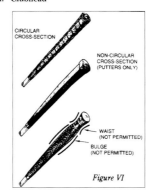

Figure VI

Dimensions. The dimensions of a clubhead are measured, with the clubhead in its normal address position, on horizontal lines between vertical projections of the outermost points of (i) the heel and the toe and (ii) the face and the back (See Fig. VII, dimension A). If the outermost point of the heel is not clearly defined, it is deemed to be 0.625 inches (16mm) above the horizontal plane on which the club is resting in its normal address position (See Fig. VII, dimension B).

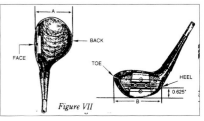

Figure VII

Plain in Shape. The clubhead shall be generally plain in shape. All parts shall be rigid, structural in nature and functional.
    It is not practicable to define plain in shape precisely and comprehensively but features which are deemed to be in breach of this requirement and are therefore not permitted include:
(a)   holes through the head,
(b)   transparent material added for other than decorative or structural purposes,
(c)   appendages to the main body of the head such as knobs, plates, rods or fins, for the purpose of meeting dimensional specifications, for aiming or for any other purpose. Exceptions may be made for putters.
    Any furrows in or runners on the sole shall not extend into the face.
4-1e. Club Face
General. The material and construction of the face shall not have the effect at impact of a spring, or impart significantly more spin to the ball than a standard steel face, or have any other effect which would unduly influence the movement of the ball.
Impact Area Rougness and Material. Except for markings, specified in the following paragraphs, the surface roughness within the area where impact is intended (the "impact area") must not exceed that of decorative sandblasting, or of fine milling.
    The impact area must be of a single material. Exceptions may be made for wooden clubs (see Fig. VIII, illustrative impact area).

Figure VIII

"Impact Area" Markings. Markings in the impact area must not have sharp edges or raised lips as determined by a finger rest. Grooves or punch marks in the impact area must meet the following specifications:
(i)   **Grooves.** A series of straight grooves with diverging sides and a symmetrical cross-section may be used (see Fig. IX). The width and cross-section must be consistent across the face of the club and along the length of the grooves. Any rounding of groove edges shall be in the form of a radius which does not exceed 0.020 inches (0.5mm). The width of the grooves shall not exceed 0.035 inches (0.9mm), using the 30 degree method of

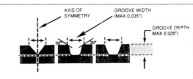

EXAMPLES OF PERMISSIBLE GROOVE CROSS-SECTIONS

Figure IX

Accumulation of Leaves (or the like)
Declaring such areas to be "ground under repair" (Rule 25). The Committee may, by Local Rule, deny relief from interference with a player's stance by such areas – see Note to Rule 25-1a.
Note: For relief from aeration holes see Specimen Local Rule 8 in Part B of this Appendix.

4. Extreme Wetness, Mud, Poor Conditions and Protection of Course
a. Lifting an Embedded Ball, Cleaning
Where the ground is unusually soft, the Committee may, by temporary Local Rule, allow the lifting of a ball which is embedded in its own pitch-mark in the ground in an area "through the green" which is not "closely mown" (Rule 25-2) if it is satisfied that the proper playing of the game would otherwise be prevented. The Local Rule shall be for that day only or for a short period, and if practicable shall be confined to specified areas. The Committee shall withdraw the Local Rule as soon as conditions warrant and should not print it on the score card.

In similarly adverse conditions, the Committee may, by temporary Local Rule, permit the cleaning of a ball "through the green".

b. "Preferred Lies" and "Winter Rules"
Adverse conditions, including the poor condition of the course or the existence of mud, are sometimes so general, particularly during winter months, that the Committee may decide to grant relief by temporary Local Rule either to protect the course or to promote fair and pleasant play. Such Local Rule shall be withdrawn as soon as conditions warrant.

5. Environmentally-Sensitive Areas
When the Committee is required to prohibit play from environmentally-sensitive areas which are on or adjoin the course, it should make a Local Rule clarifying the relief procedure.

An environmentally-sensistive area is an area so declared by an appropriate authority, entry into and/or play from which is prohibited for environmental reasons. Such an area may be defined as ground under repair, a water hazard, a lateral water hazard or out of bounds at the discretion of the Committee provided that, in the case of an environmentally-sensitive area which has been defined as a water hazard or a lateral water hazard, the area is, by Definition, a water hazard.
Note: The Committee may not declare an area to be environmentally-sensistive.

A specimen Local Rule is detailed in "Decisions on the Rules of Golf".

Other matters which the Committee could cover by Local Rule include:

6. Water Hazards
a. Lateral Water Hazards
Clarifying the status of sections of water hazards which may be lateral water hazards (Rule 26).

b. Provisional Ball
Permitting play of a provisional ball for a ball which may be in a water hazard of such character that it would be impracticable to determine whether the ball is in the hazard or to do so would unduly delay play. In such a case, if a provisional ball is played and the original ball is in a water hazard, the player may play the original ball as it lies or continue the provisional ball in play, but he may not proceed under Rule 26-1.

7. Defining Bounds and Margins
Specifying means used to define out of bounds, hazards, water hazards, lateral water hazards and ground under repair.

8. Dropping Zones
Establishing special areas in which balls may or shall be dropped when it is not feasible or practicable to proceed exactly in conformity with Rule 24-2b (Immovable Obstruction), Rule 25-1b or Rule 25-1c (Ground Under Repair), Rule 25-3 (Wrong Putting Green), Rule 26-1 (Water Hazards and Lateral Water Hazards) or Rule 28 (Ball Unplayable)

9. Priority on the Course
The Committee may make regulations governing Priority on the Course (see Etiquette).

PART B SPECIMEN LOCAL RULES

Within the policy set out in Part A of this Appendix, the Committee may adopt a Specimen Local Rule by referring, on a score card or notice board, to the examples given below. However, Specimen Local Rules 5, 6 or 7 should not be printed or referred to on a score card as they are all of limited duration.

1. Fixed Sprinkler Heads
All fixed sprinkler heads are immovable obstructions and relief from interference by them may be obtained under Rule 24-2. In addition, if such an obstruction on or within two club-lengths of the putting green of the hole being played intervenes on the line of play between the ball and the hole, the player may obtain relief, without penalty, as follows:

If the ball lies off the putting green but not in a hazard and is within two club-lengths of the intervening obstruction, it may be lifted, cleaned and dropped at the nearest point to where the ball lay which (a) is not nearer the hole, (b) avoids such intervention and (c) is not in a hazard or on a putting green.

PENALTY FOR BREACH OF LOCAL RULE: *Match play – Loss of Hole; Stroke play – Two strokes.*

2. Stones in Bunkers
Stones in bunkers are movable obstructions (Rule 24-1 applies)

3. Protection of Young Trees
Protection of young trees identified by __________________ . If such a tree interferes with a player's stance or the area of his intended swing, the ball must be lifted, without penalty, and dropped in accordance with the procedure prescribed in Rule 24-2b(i) (Immovable Obstruction). The ball may be cleaned when so lifted.

PENALTY FOR BREACH OF LOCAL RULE
Match play – Loss of hole; Stroke play – Two strokes.

4. Ground Under Repair: Play Prohibited
If a player's ball lies in an area of "ground under repair" from which play is prohibited, or if such an area of "ground under repair" interferes with the player's stance or the area of his intended swing the player must take relief under Rule 25-1.

PENALTY FOR BREACH OF LOCAL RULE
Match play – Loss of hole; Stroke play – Two strokes.

5. Lifting an Embedded Ball
(Specify the area if practicable) . . . through the green, a ball embedded in its own pitch-mark in ground other than sand may be lifted, cleaned and dropped, without penalty, as near as possible to the spot where it lay but not nearer the hole.

PENALTY FOR BREACH OF LOCAL RULE: *Match play – Loss of hole; Stroke play – Two strokes.*

6. Cleaning Ball
(Specify the area if practicable) . . . through the green a ball may be lifted, cleaned and replaced without penalty.
Note: The position of the ball shall be marked before it is lifted under this Local Rule – see Rule 20-1.

7. "Preferred Lies" and "Winter Rules"
A ball lying on any "closely mown area" through the green may, without penalty, be moved or may be lifted, cleaned and placed within six inches of where it originally lay, but not nearer the hole. After the ball has been so moved or placed, it is in play.

PENALTY FOR BREACH OF LOCAL RULE:
Match play – Loss of hole; Stroke play – Two strokes.

8. Aeration Holes
If a ball comes to rest in an aeration hole, the player may, without penalty, lift the ball and clean it. Through the green, the player shall drop the ball as near as possible to where it lay, but not nearer the hole. On the putting green, the player shall place the ball at the nearest spot not nearer the hole which avoids such situation.

PENALTY FOR BREACH OF LOCAL RULE: *Match play – Loss of hole; Stroke play – Two strokes.*

PART C CONDITIONS OF THE COMPETITION

Rule 33-1 provides, "The Committee shall lay down the conditions under which a competition is to be played". Such conditions should include many matters such as method of entry, eligibility, number of rounds to be played, settling ties, etc. which it is not appropriate to deal with in the Rules of Golf or this Appendix. Detailed information regarding such conditions is provided in "Decisions on the Rules of Golf" under Rule 33-1.

However, there are seven matters which might be covered in the Conditions of the Competition to which the Committee's attention is specifically drawn by way of a Note to the appropriate Rule. These are:

1. Specification of the Ball (Note to Rule 5-1)
a. List of Conforming Golf Balls
Arising from the regulations for ball-testing under Rule 5-1, a List of Conforming Golf Balls will be issued from time to time.

It is recommended that the List should be applied to all National and County (or equivalent) Championships and to all top-class events when restricted to low handicap players. In order to apply the List to a particular competition the Committee must lay this down in the Conditions of the Competition. This should be referred to in the Entry Form, and also a notice should be displayed on the Club notice board and at the 1st Tee along the following lines:

..............(Name of Event)...........................

..............(Date and Club).........................

"The Ball (Note to Rule 5-1).
The ball the player uses shall be named on the current List of Conforming Golf Balls issued by the Royal and Ancient Golf Club of St. Andrews."

A penalty statement will be required and must be either:

(a) "PENALTY FOR BREACH OF CONDITION: *Disqualification.*"

or

(b) "PENALTY FOR BREACH OF CONDITION: *Match play – Loss of each hole at which a breach occurred. Stroke play – Two strokes for each hole at which a breach occurred.*"

If option (b) is adopted this only applies to use of a ball which, whilst not on the List of Conforming Golf Balls, does conform to the specifications set forth in Rule 5 and Appendix III. The penalty for use of a ball which does not so conform is disqualification.

b. One Ball Condition
If it is desired to prohibit changing brands and types of golf balls during a stipulated round, the following condition is recommended:

"Limitation on Balls Used During Round: (Note to Rule 5-1).
(i) "One Ball" Condition
During a stipulated round, the ball the player uses must be of the same brand and type as detailed by a single entry on the current List of Conforming Golf Balls.
PENALTY FOR BREACH OF CONDITION: *Match Play – At the conclusion of the hole at which the breach is discovered, the state of the match shall be adjusted by deducting one hole for each hole at which a breach occurred; maximum deduction per round: Two holes. Stroke Play – Two strokes for each hole at which any breach occurred; maximum penalty per round; Four strokes.*
(ii) Procedure When Breach Discovered
When a player discovers that he has used a ball in breach of this condition, he shall abandon that ball before playing from the next teeing ground and complete the round using a proper ball; otherwise, the player shall be disqualified. If discovery is made during play of a hole and the player elects to substitute a proper ball before completing that hole, the player shall place a proper ball on the spot where the ball used in breach of the condition lay."
Note: In Club events it is recommended that no such condition be applied.

2. Time of Starting (Note to Rule 6-3a)
If the Committee wishes to act in accordance with the Note, the following wording is recommended:

"If the player arrives at his starting point, ready to play, within five minutes after his starting time, in the absence of circumstances which warrant waiving the penalty of disqualification as provided in Rule 33-7, the penalty for failure to start on time is loss of the first hole to be played in match play or two strokes in stroke play. Penalty for lateness beyond five minutes is disqualification."

3. Pace of Play
The Committee may lay down pace of play guidelines, to help prevent slow play, in accordance with Note 2 to Rule 6-7.

4. Suspension of Play Due to a Dangerous Situation (Note to Rule 6-8b)
If the Committee wishes to act in accordance with the Note, the following wording is recommended:

"When play is suspended by the Committee for a dangerous situation (e.g. lightning, tornados, etc.) if the players in a match or group are between the play of two holes, they shall not resume play until the Committee has ordered a resumption of play. If they are in the process of playing a hole, they shall discontinue play immediately and shall not thereafter resume play until the Committee has ordered a resumption of play.

The signal for suspending play due to a dangerous situation will be ....

5. Practice

The Committee may make regulations governing practice in accordance with the Note to Rule 7-1, Exception (c) to Rule 7-2, Note 2 to Rule 7 and Rule 33-2c.

6. Advice in Team Competitions

If the Committee wishes to act in accordance with the Note, the following wording is recommended:

"In accordance with the Note to Rule 8 of the Rules of Golf each team may appoint one person (in addition to the persons from whom advice may be asked under that Rule) who may give advice to members of that team. Such person *[if it is desired to insert any restriction on who may be nominated insert such restriction here]* shall be identified to the Committee before giving advice."

7. New Holes

The Committee may provide, in accordance with the Note to Rule 33-2b, that the holes and teeing grounds for a single round competition, being held on more than one day, may be differently situated on each day.

APPENDICES II AND III

Any design in a club or ball which is not covered by Rules 4 and 5 and Appendices II and III, or which might significantly change the nature of the game, will be ruled on by the Royal and Ancient Golf Club of St. Andrews and the United States Golf Association.

APPENDIX II

Design of Clubs

Clubs must not be substantially different from the traditional and customary form and make.

Rule 4-1 prescribes general regulations for their design. The following paragraphs, which provide some specifications and clarify how Rule 4-1 is interpreted, should be read in conjunction with that Rule.

Where a club, or part of a club, is required to have some specific property, this means that it must be designed and manufactured with the intention of having that property. The finished club or part must have that property within manufacturing tolerances appropriate to the material used.

4-1a. General

Adjustability – Exception for Putters. Clubs other than putters shall not be designed to be adjustable except for weight.

Some other forms of adjustability are permitted in the design of a putter, provided that:

(i) the adjustment cannot be readily made;
(ii) all adjustable parts are firmly fixed and there is no reasonable likelihood of them working loose during a round; and
(iii) all configurations of adjustment conform with the Rules.

The disqualification penalty for purposely changing the playing characteristics of a club during a stipulated round (Rule 4-2) applies to all clubs including a putter.

Note: It is recommended that all putters with adjustable parts be submitted to the Royal and Ancient Golf Club of St. Andrews for a ruling.

4-1b. Shaft

Straightness. The shaft shall be straight from the top of the grip to a point not more than 5 inches (127 mm) above the sole, measured from the point where the shaft ceases to be straight along the axis of the bent part of the shaft and the neck and/or socket (See Fig. 1);

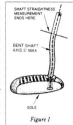

Figure I

Length. The overall length of the club shall be at least 18 inches (457 mm) measured from the top of the grip along the axis of the shaft or a straight line extension of it to the sole of the club.

Alignment. When the club is in its normal address position the shaft shall be so aligned that:

(i) the projection of the straight part of the shaft on to the vertical plane through the toe and heel shall diverge from the vertical by at least ten degrees (See Fig. II);

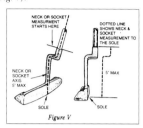

Figure II

(ii) the projection of the straight part of the shaft on to the vertical plane along the intended line of play shall not diverge from the vertical by more than 20 degrees (See Fig. III).

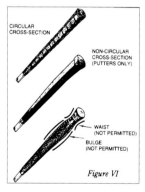

Figure III

Except for putters, all of the heel portion of the club shall lie within 0.625 inches (16 mm) of the plane containing the axis of the straight part of the shaft and the intended (horizontal) line of play (See Fig. IV).

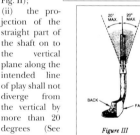

Figure IV

Bending and Twisting Properties. At any point along its length, the shaft shall:
(i) bend in such a way that the deflection is the same regardless of how the shaft is rotated about its longitudinal axis; and
(ii) twist the same amount in both directions.

Attachment to Clubhead. The shaft shall be attached to the clubhead at the heel either directly or through a neck and/or socket. The length from the top of the neck and/or socket to the sole of the club shall not exceed 5 inches (127 mm), measured along the axis of, and following any bend in, the neck and/or socket (See Fig. V).

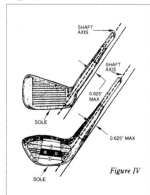

Figure V

Exception for Putters: The shaft or neck or socket of a putter may be fixed at any point in the head.

4-1c. Grip (See Fig. VI)
(i) For clubs other than putters the grip must be circular in cross-section, except that a continuous, straight, slightly raised rib may be incorporated along the full length of the grip, and a slightly indented spiral is permitted on a wrapped grip or a replica of one.
(ii) A putter grip may have a non-circular cross-section, provided the cross-section has no concavity, is symmetrical and remains generally similar throughout the length of the grip.
(iii) The grip may be tapered but must not have any bulge or waist. Its cross-sectional dimension measured in any direction must not exceed 1.75 inches (45 mm).
(iv) For clubs other than putters the axis of the grip must coincide with the axis of the shaft.
(v) A putter may have more than one grip, provided each is circular in cross-section and the axis of each coincides with the axis of the shaft.

4-1d. Clubhead

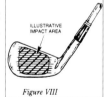

Figure VI

Dimensions. The dimensions of a clubhead are measured, with the clubhead in its normal address position, on horizontal lines between vertical projections of the outermost points of (i) the heel and the toe and (ii) the face and the back (See Fig. VII, dimension A). If the outermost point of the heel is not clearly defined, it is deemed to be 0.625 inches (16mm) above the horizontal plane on which the club is resting in its normal address position (See Fig. VII, dimension B).

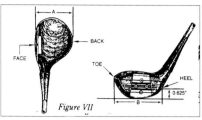

Figure VII

Plain in Shape. The clubhead shall be generally plain in shape. All parts shall be rigid, structural in nature and functional.

It is not practicable to define plain in shape precisely and comprehensively but features which are deemed to be in breach of this requirement and are therefore not permitted include:
(a) holes through the head,
(b) transparent material added for other than decorative or structural purposes,
(c) appendages to the main body of the head such as knobs, plates, rods or fins, for the purpose of meeting dimensional specifications, for aiming or for any other purpose. Exceptions may be made for putters.

Any furrows in or runners on the sole shall not extend into the face.

4-1e. Club Face

General. The material and construction of the face shall not have the effect at impact of a spring, or impart significantly more spin to the ball than a standard steel face, or have any other effect which would unduly influence the movement of the ball.

Impact Area Roughness and Material. Except for markings specified in the following paragraphs, the surface roughness within the area where impact is intended (the "impact area") must not exceed that of decorative sandblasting, or of fine milling.

The impact area must be of a single material. Exceptions may be made for wooden clubs (see Fig. VIII, illustrative impact area).

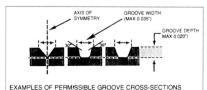

Figure VIII

"Impact Area" Markings. Markings in the impact area must not have sharp edges or raised lips as determined by a finger rest. Grooves or punch marks in the impact area must meet the following specifications:
(i) **Grooves.** A series of straight grooves with diverging sides and a symmetrical cross-section may be used (see Fig. IX). The width and cross-section must be consistent across the face of the club and along the length of the grooves. Any rounding of groove edges shall be in the form of a radius which does not exceed 0.020 inches (0.5mm). The width of the grooves shall not exceed 0.035 inches (0.9mm), using the 30 degree method of

EXAMPLES OF PERMISSIBLE GROOVE CROSS-SECTIONS

Figure IX

measurement on file with the Royal and Ancient Golf Club of St. Andrews. The distance between edges of adjacent grooves must not be less than three times the width of a groove, and not less than 0.075 inches (1.9mm). The depth of a groove must not exceed 0.020 inches (0.5mm).

(ii) **Punch Marks.** Punch marks may be used. The area of any such mark must not exceed 0.0044 square inches (2.8 sq.mm). A mark must not be closer to an adjacent mark than 0.168 inches (4.3mm) measured from centre to centre. The depth of a punch mark must not exceed 0.040 inches (1.0mm). If punch marks are used in combination with grooves, a punch mark must not be closer to a groove than 0.168 inches (4.3mm), measured from centre to centre.

Decorative Markings. The centre of the impact area may be indicated by a design within the boundary of a square whose sides are 0.375 inches (9.5mm) in length. Such a design must not unduly influence the movement of the ball. Decorative markings are permitted outside the impact area.

Non-metallic Club Face Markings. The above specifications apply to clubs on which the impact area of the face is of metal or a material of similar hardness. They do not apply to clubs with faces made of other materials and whose loft angle is 24 degrees or less, but markings which could unduly influence the movement of the ball are prohibited. Clubs with this type of face and a loft angle exceeding 24 degrees may have grooves of maximum width 0.040 inches (1.00mm) and maximum depth 1½ times the groove width, but must otherwise conform to the markings specifications above.

Putter Face Markings. The specifications above with regard to club face markings and surface roughness do not apply to putters.

APPENDIX III

THE BALL

a. Weight
The weight of the ball shall not be greater than 1.620 ounces avoirdupois (45.93 gm).

b. Size
The diameter of the ball shall be not less than 1.680 inches (42.67mm). This specification will be satisfied if, under its own weight, a ball falls through a 1.680 inches diameter ring gauge in fewer than 25 out of 100 randomly selected positions, the test being carried out at a temperature of $23\pm1^{\circ}C$.

c. Spherical Symmetry
The ball must not be designed, manufactured or intentionally modified to have properties which differ from those of a spherically symmetrical ball.

d. Initial Velocity
The velocity of the ball shall not be greater than 250 feet (76.2m) per second when measured on apparatus approved by the Royal and Ancient Golf Club of St. Andrews. A maximum tolerance of 2% will be allowed. The temperature of the ball when tested shall be $23\pm1^{\circ}C$.

e. Overall Distance Standard
A brand of golf ball, when tested on apparatus approved by the Royal and Ancient Golf Club of St. Andrews under the conditions set forth in the Overall Distance Standard for golf balls on file with the Royal and Ancient Golf Club of St. Andrews, shall not cover an average distance in carry and roll exceeding 280 yards (256 metres) plus a tolerance of 6%.
Note: The 6% tolerance will be reduced to a minimum of 4% as test techniques are improved.

RULES OF GOLF COMMITTEE 1996/97

D. I. Pepper (Chairman)
I. R. H. Pattinson (Deputy Chairman)
N. J. Crichton
J. M. Kippax
M. C. Tate
P. D. Montgomery
M. E. Baird
G. H. Smith
C. J. L. Strachan
R. M. E. Davitt
D. K. Rae
M. Yates

ADVISORY MEMBERS OF THE RULES OF GOLF COMMITTEE

E. J. H. Yong	Asia-Pacific Golf Confederation
J. Hopkins	Australian Golf Union
J. A. Cook	Royal Canadian Golf Association
I. E. M. Hughes	Council of National Golf Unions
J. A. Moreira	European Golf Association
H. Goldscheider	European Golf Association
T. Kawata	Japan Golf Association
Mrs E. Earnshaw	Ladies' Golf Union
F. I. Henderson	New Zealand Golf Association
M. M. Pinto	South African Golf Federation
J. V. Garasino	South American Golf Federation
Dr T. Holland	United States Golf Association

CHAIRMEN AND DEPUTY CHAIRMEN OF THE RULES OF GOLF COMMITTEE (1897-1997)

DATE	CHAIRMAN	DEPUTY CHAIRMAN
1897-1903	B. Hall Blyth	
1903-1913	Captain W. H. Burn	
1913-1921	John L. Low	
1921-1946	Angus V. Hambro	
1946-1949	Bernard Darwin*	Col. T. J. Mitchell
1949-1952	Dr H. Gardiner-Hill	Lt. Col. J. Inglis (1949-1953)
1952-1955	Lt Col. C. O. Hezlet	Dr. J. Lawson (1953-1955)
1955-1957	J. L. Mitchell	D. F. McCurrach
1957-1959	G. A. Hill	D. F. Simpson
1959-1963	G. H. Micklem	D. F. McCurrach (1959-1961)
		R. MacLeod (1961-1963)
1963-1964	R. MacLeod	J. S. Lawson
1964-1968	D. N. V. Smith	D. F. Simpson (1964-1965)
		J. S. Lawson (1965-1968)
1968-1972	J. S. Lawson	G. R. Cockburn
1972-1976	G. R. Cockburn	F. R. Furber
1976-1980	F. R. Furber	D. L. Hayes
1980-1984	D. L. Hayes	J. L. S. Pasquill
1984-1985	G. Huddy	A. C. Caithness (1984-1988)
1985-1988	W. J. F. Bryce	
1988-1990	Dr D. M. Marsh	J. S. Scrivener
1990-1995	J. S. Scrivener	G. S. Lowden (1990-1991)
		J. J. N. Caplan (1991-1993)
		D. I. Pepper (1993-1994)
		N. M. Stephens (1994-1996)
1995-	D. I. Pepper	I. R. H. Pattinson (1996-)

* Office of Deputy Chairman created for first time.

CHAIRMEN OF THE IMPLEMENTS & BALL COMMITTEE (1974-1997)

DATE	CHAIRMAN
1974-1977	D. L. Hayes
1977-1978	G. R. Cockburn
1978-1982	G. Huddy
1982-1990	R. G. Ames
1990-1995	J. G. Coulter
1995-	W. J. F. Bryce

CHAIRMEN OF THE AMATEUR STATUS COMMITTEE (1966-1997)

DATE	CHAIRMAN
1966-1968	G. H. Micklem
1968-1970	C. D. Lawrie
1970-1975	J. E. Behrend
1975-1979	M. F. Bonallack
1979-1981	A. Sinclair
1981-1985	B. H. G. Chapman
1985-1989	W. F. Callander
1989-1993	M. A. Boddington
1993-1996	I. W. L. Webb
1996-	A. J. Hill

QUADRENNIAL RULES CONFERENCE, CHESTER, MAY 1983

Back row John Glover, Grant Spaeth, Niel Loudon, Bill Battle, Cecil Evans, Marion Farmer, Jim Kellie, Alan Caithness, Jens Wester-Andersen, Ivar Brostrom, **Seated** Will Nicholson, P. J. Boatwright Jr, Bill Williams (Chairman USGA), Denis Hayes (Chairman R&A), John Pasquill, Michael Bonallack

NOT IN THE SPIRIT OF THE GAME *(see page 128)*

A drouthy lot, the curling crew!
Their broomstick tops they can unscrew
And fill the shaft with barley-broo;
 Does 'soop' mean 'sweep' or 'sup'?
Now, could a thirsty golfer use,
Without offence, a putter whose
True-temper shaft was filled with booze
To keep his spirits up?

Rule 2-2a ('the club' defined)
Bans any club that's been designed
To be adjustable we find
 (Except, of course, for weight);
And each component part must be
So fixed that we may plainly see
The club is in entirety
A unit integrate.

It might be said that if the knop
Which plugs the shaft and seals the top
Could be unscrewed this would not stop
The club from being 'one';
And if the top 'can be unscrewed'
This phrase could scarcely be construed
As 'is adjustable'. How shrewd!
 But wait; we haven't done.

For, if a putter-shaft be filled
With liquor (malted or distilled)
And at some hole a tot be swilled
To wet one's dusty clay,

Rule 2-2b now operates;
One must not change (it clearly states)
The club's inherent playing traits
While play is under way.

You must admit (here lies the craft)
Each tiny drop of whisky quaffed
Would change the balance of the shaft
 By lessening its weight.
Nor is that all! From top to toe
Within the shaft a lively flow
Of liquor, sloshing to and fro,
Each swing would generate.

And so, on balance, we're inclined
To rule against a club designed
For holding drink of any kind;
 A putter most of all.
For just suppose, in rage or grief,
One broke the shaft, it's our belief
Rule 32 gives no relief
From casual alcohol!

Stewart Lawson

Since the above was written the Rules have been renumbered. The Club is now under Rule 4 and Casual Water under Rule 25. The golfer's comment on the answer given was that the R&A were 'a bunch of kill-joys'!

HOW WOULD YOU RULE? THE OFFICIAL DECISIONS

Page 30 Your partner's air-shot is a stroke with a wrong ball in breach of Rule 15-2, for which the penalty in match play is loss of hole.

Therefore, your side's next stroke will be from the next tee and Rule 29-1 determines whose turn it is to play!

Page 39 No. The player must proceed under Rule 27-1 (see Decision 1-4/1).

Page 47 Each player is an outside agency in relation to the other.

Under Rule 19-1a, A must play his ball as it lies, without penalty. B incurs no penalty for striking A's ball (see Decision 15/2), but the stroke counts. (See also Decision 19-1/2).

Page 65 No. However, the players may be subject to penalty under Rule 6-7 (Undue Delay).

Page 67 In equity (Rule 1-4), the player should place her ball in an equivalent position in relation to the newly cut hole.

Page 89 Yes. The clubhouse is an immovable obstruction. However, any part of it designed to be movable, such as a window or door, may be moved to any position if this can be done without undue delay (Rule 6-7). (See Decision 24-2b/14).

Page 109 No. In either case the player incurs a penalty of two strokes (See Rule 15-3 and Decision 15-3/2).

Page 127 Yes, in equity (Rule 1-4).

Page 165 The player has not made a stroke because his intention to strike the ball ceased during his down-swing. (See Decision 14/1.5).

The 'Suggestion Box' at the St Andrews Course, Hamilton Golf Club, New Zealand.

The 'Suggestion Box' at the St Andrews Course, Hamilton Golf Club, New Zealand.